Carl von Clausewitz's **On War**
A Biography

Current and forthcoming titles in the
Books That Changed the World series:

The Bible by Karen Armstrong
Machiavelli's *The Prince* by Philip Bobbitt
Plato's *Republic* by Simon Blackburn
Darwin's *Origin of Species* by Janet Browne
Thomas Paine's *Rights of Man* by Christopher Hitchens
The Qur'an by Bruce Lawrence
Homer's *The Iliad and the Odyssey* by Alberto Manguel
On The Wealth of Nations by P. J. O'Rourke
Marx's *Das Kapital* by Francis Wheen

Clausewitz's
On War
A Biography

HEW STRACHAN

Atlantic Monthly Press
New York

First published in Great Britain in 2007 by Atlantic Books

Printed in the United States of America

FIRST AMERICAN EDITION

Library of Congress Cataloging-in-Publication Data

Strachan, Hew.
    Clausewitz's On War : a biography / Hew Strachan.
        p. cm.
    Includes bibliographical references and index.
    Contents: The reality of war—The writing of On war—The nature of war—
The theory of war.
    ISBN-10: 0-87113-956-1
    ISBN-13: 978-0-87113-956-6
    1. Clausewitz, Carl von, 1780–1831. Vom Kriege.   2. War.   3. Military art
and science.   4. Politics and war.   I. Title.

U102.C6643S72 2007
355.02—dc22   2006052286

Design by Richard Marston

Atlantic Monthly Press
an imprint of Grove/Atlantic, Inc.
841 Broadway
New York, NY 10003

Distributed by Publishers Group West

www.groveatlantic.com

07 08 09 10 11   10 9 8 7 6 5 4 3 2 1

CONTENTS

ACKNOWLEDGEMENTS

I was invited to write this book at the end of 2003, when I had just returned from giving a series of lectures and seminars on Clausewitz at the Royal Norwegian Air Force Academy in Trondheim. Not for the first time, the fertility of Clausewitz's thinking had left my mind buzzing with ideas and I accepted the offer with alacrity. My first debt, therefore, is to those responsible for entertaining me in Norway, and especially to Nils Naastad, Ole-Jørgen Maao and above all Harald Hoiback, who made several suggestions for the book's improvement. Since then I have acquired an obligation to Andreas Herberg-Rothe. In March 2005 he and I organized a conference on Clausewitz in the twenty-first century, under the auspices of the Oxford Leverhulme Programme on the Changing Character of War, whose director I am. I should take this opportunity to record my thanks to the Trustees of the Leverhulme Foundation for their extraordinarily generous support of the study of war at Oxford. Hamish Scott, a friend of long standing, became a neighbour as I was writing: his book, *The Birth of a Great Power System*

1740–1815, was my *vade mecum* through Clausewitz's Europe.

Writing this book has cost my family another summer holiday, and I thank my wife Pamela from the bottom of my heart; she has even read and commented on this one. My brother Gavin Strachan has relieved me of obligations, both filial and rural.

A NOTE ON TRANSLATIONS AND EDITIONS

On War, or *Vom Kriege*, was first published in three volumes by Ferdinand Dümmler in Berlin between 1832 and 1834. It then appeared in a second edition with some alterations to the text as well as minor corrections in 1853–7. A third edition followed in 1867–9. Most translations, including the first English translation of 1873, by J. J. Graham, revised by F. N. Maude in 1908 (Kegan Paul, Trench, Trubner & Co.), were derived from the second edition, not the first.

In 1952 Werner Hahlweg restored the original text of the first edition, in what was by then the sixteenth edition (Bonn, Dümmler). This is the German version I have used. Hahlweg provides a full scholarly apparatus (unlike any of the English editions), and his text is now in its nineteenth edition.

In 1976 Michael Howard and Peter Paret published a new English translation based on the first German edition. As this is the version which is now standard in the English-speaking world, quotations from *On War* in what follows are – unless otherwise specified – derived from it (although their spelling is anglicized where appropriate) and page references are to the first edition, published by Princeton University Press.

In the process of comparing the German text with the English translations, I have found myself diverging from some of the interpretations embraced by Michael Howard and Peter Paret. Readers will therefore also find references to the two earlier English-language translations, even if they are not based on the first German edition. J. J. Graham's translation of 1873 was dominant until 1976, especially in the version abridged by Anatol Rapoport and published by Penguin in 1968. Both Graham's translation and the shorter Penguin edition are in print at the time of writing. So, too, after a long interval, is the version most faithful to the original German, that of O. J. Matthijs Jolles, first published by Random House in New York in 1943. I have used the edition published by the *Infantry Journal* in Washington in 1950.

There is no standard system of referencing Clausewitz, and the different editions in many languages result in pagination which is anything but uniform. Joachim Niemeyer produced a concordance to the German editions of *On War* in his edition of Clausewitz's *Historische Briefe über die grossen Kriegereignisse im Oktober 1806* (Bonn, Dümmler, 1977). Some chapters of *On War* cover several pages, and simply giving book and chapter numbers (which are consistent across all editions) is insufficient aid to the scholar. I have therefore adopted a reference system that gives three numbers. The first is the number of the book, the second is the number of the chapter, and the third is the number of the page of the edition from which I am quoting. If the edition is not specified, then the reference is to the Howard and Paret version in its original edition, as published by Princeton University Press in 1976. Where I have been unhappy with their translation and used another, or have referred to the German because I have found no other English translation wholly satisfactory, I have made that clear.

INTRODUCTION

In 1975, six years after returning from his last tour of duty in Vietnam, Colonel (as he was then) Colin Powell went to the US National War College. A year later, Princeton University Press brought out a fresh English-language edition of Carl von Clausewitz's *Vom Kriege*, or *On War*, first published posthumously in German in three volumes between 1832 and 1834. Two of the most distinguished historians of their generation, Michael Howard and Peter Paret, were responsible for the translation. Howard had fought with distinction in the Second World War: Clausewitz appealed to him as a soldier writing for other soldiers. His aim was an English version that soldiers themselves would read, and, just in case they did not, Bernard Brodie, a star of the strategic studies firmament of the nuclear age, concluded the volume with a short summary of the text. The Princeton edition of *On War* has proved far more successful than the German original ever was. It not only rendered Clausewitz's prose in language that is readable and graphic (as is the original), but also gave the text an inner unity which many of its readers had denied it possessed.

Over the last thirty years American soldiers in particular have responded to Howard's hopes.

One of them was Colonel Powell. He described *On War* as 'a beam of light from the past, still illuminating present-day military quandaries'. Confused by the disintegration in Vietnam of the army he loved, and alarmed by the gulf that had opened between it and the society it served, he found explanations for what had gone wrong in *On War*. 'Clausewitz's greatest lesson for my profession was that the soldier, for all his patriotism, valor, and skill, forms just one leg in a triad. Without all three legs engaged, the military, the government, and the people, the enterprise cannot stand.'[1] Powell was not alone in using Clausewitz to explain what had gone wrong in Vietnam. In 1981 Colonel Harry Summers, Jr, prepared a study for the US Army War College entitled *On Strategy: A critical analysis of the Vietnam war*. Published in 1982, it had already been printed three times by 1983. Summers applied *On War* (as translated by Howard and Paret) to identify the 'missing link' in US strategy – 'the failure to address the question of "how" to use military means to achieve a political end'. Summers, like Powell, highlighted Clausewitz's 'trinity', which he, also like Powell, maintained was made up of army, government and people. Feeling, too, that he had to justify his use of a text that had been published 150 years before, Summers insisted 'that this is the most *modern* source available'.[2]

Summers had no cause to be so defensive. In 1983 Powell became the senior military assistant to Caspar

Weinberger, the Secretary of Defense in Ronald Reagan's administration. Like Powell, Weinberger was determined to put the army back on its feet, and he too found inspiration from *On War*. In November 1984 he laid down criteria for the use of American troops abroad: 'As Clausewitz wrote, "No one starts a war – or rather, no one in his senses ought to do so – without first being clear in his mind what he intends to achieve by that war, and how he intends to conduct it."'[3] Failing to do this in Vietnam was, in Powell's words, 'mistake number one'. It 'led to Clausewitz's rule number two. Political leaders must set a war's objectives, while armies achieve them.'

Powell and Weinberger were attracted to Clausewitz precisely because he seemed to be so clear about the relationship between war and policy. However, in 1989 the collapse of the Soviet Union left the political context fluid and even opaque. Powell was appointed Chairman of the Joint Chiefs of Staff just as the United States' military found itself without an equal. In 1992, as Bosnian Serbs slaughtered Muslims in the former Yugoslavia, America's public called for its government to use military intervention. Powell's reaction was to reiterate the Weinberger doctrine, stressing the need for clear political objectives before American ground troops were committed in the Balkans. But he went further: he rejected the use of 'limited force', stating that 'decisive means and results are always to be preferred'.[4] This too was a sentiment whose origins were Clausewitzian.

The American army's other intellectual response to defeat in Vietnam had been to rethink its operational doctrine for the conduct of war, a process in which it took the German army as a model. Between 1871 and 1945 the German general staff had embraced what it called a 'strategy of annihilation', the achievement of a victory on the battlefield so decisive and so speedy that it would determine the political outcome. It was an idea which it traced to Clausewitz. Therefore two currents – one embracing the political purpose of war and the other the way it should be fought, but both drawing on a Clausewitzian pedigree – converged in the Powell doctrine of 1992. In the ensuing decade, the US army, increasingly conscious of its military superiority, focused on the second current, 'decisive means and results', to the exclusion of the first. The planning of the Iraq War of 2003 revealed that an updated version of the German 'strategy of annihilation' had subsumed Clausewitz's 'rule number one', as ironically Colin Powell – now Secretary of State – discovered. Tommy Franks, Commander-in-Chief of the United States Central Command, was almost wilful in his pursuit of rapid operational success at the expense of long-term political goals. For him 'the maxims of the Prussian strategist Carl von Clausewitz had dictated that mass – concentrated formations of troops and guns – was the key to victory. To achieve victory, Clausewitz advised, a military power must mass its forces at the enemy's "center of gravity".'[5]

Franks had been a one-star general in Operation Desert Storm, the war against Iraq in 1990–91. Then the forces of the United States and its allies had been able to apply the operational doctrine developed after Vietnam, and designed to counter the Soviet Union in the 1980s, to devastating effect. The question that dominated the aftermath of Desert Storm was whether its success pointed forwards or backwards. For Franks and others, focused on the operational dimension, it pointed forwards. New technologies would enable the American army to do even better next time. Franks thought that he was correcting Clausewitz (but that just showed that he had not read *On War* very carefully), when he concluded that, 'the victory in Desert Storm proved that speed has a mass of its own'. Others went even further, arguing that developments in information technology would remove the fog and uncertainty that surrounded the battlefield – what Clausewitz had called friction. It was precisely this concept that had so appealed to Michael Howard's own military experience.

Franks and his ilk saw themselves as refining Clausewitz, not rejecting him. But others – those who thought the influence of Desert Storm was retrograde – deemed *On War* to have lost its relevance. They detected changes not just in the character of war, but in its very nature. In 1991, Martin van Creveld published a book whose American edition was entitled *The Transformation of War*, and which his publishers dubbed 'the most radical reinterpretation of armed conflict since Clausewitz'. With the end of the Cold War the

Clausewitzian presumption that war is an act of force designed to fulfil the objects of policy was increasingly challenged. Clausewitz, so the argument runs, identified war with the state, not least because he presumed that only states have policies. Many of the conflicts waged since 1990 have been fought by non-state actors. Some of them fight for political objectives but do not employ the sorts of armies which Clausewitz described: instead, their tools are guerrillas and terrorists. Others wage war but not for political objectives, using conflict to mask organized crime, drug-running and money-laundering. For them the object is not peace (as it was for Clausewitz) but more war. By the late 1990s van Creveld might reasonably maintain that he had been vindicated. Mary Kaldor's *New and Old Wars*, published in 1999, drew a distinction between 'old wars', which were those that Clausewitz had studied, and the 'new wars' being waged by warlords in the Balkans, whose interests demanded the continuation of conflict, not its conclusion. For van Creveld and Kaldor, Bosnia represented what war had become, and Powell – in keeping the United States out of it because he wished to wage an 'old war' – was trapped in a typological confusion for which Clausewitz was responsible. Van Creveld took exception to what he called the 'Clausewitzian universe', not just because 'it rests on the assumption that war is made predominantly by states or, to be exact, by governments', but also because of Clausewitz's vision of war as 'trinitarian'. Like Powell and Summers, van Creveld described Clausewitz's trinity as made up of people, government and army. As we shall see, Clausewitz's trinity was not quite like that. Moreover, how central it was to the overall picture of war which animated *On War* in its entirety is open to question, as are both the relationship between war and policy and exactly what Clausewitz understood by policy.

Controversy is not new to Clausewitz; indeed, he invited it. In *On War* he took specific aim at one easy target and one difficult one. The easy one was an officer of the Prussian army, Adam Heinrich Dietrich von Bülow, who had endeavoured, not always very successfully, to explain the impact of the French Revolution of 1789 on the conduct of war. Bülow was declared insane in 1806 and died in 1807. He was not around to defend his corner in 1832. Antoine-Henri Jomini was, and indeed lived on until 1869, dying at the age of ninety. If modern strategic thought finds its roots in the nineteenth century, Jomini has a much greater claim to be its father than Clausewitz. A Swiss by nationality, he served as a staff officer with the French army of Napoleon between 1805 and 1813, writing as he went, and then devoting the rest of his career to refining his thoughts about warfare. The military academies and staff colleges that mushroomed in his lifetime and which were themselves symptomatic of the growing professional self-regard of soldiers proved ready consumers of his precepts.

Clausewitz's specific blows against Jomini in *On War* were few and glancing, rebutting what Jomini laid down as general principles. But he could be much more forthright in his other works, and became more so as he grew older. In an essay written in 1817, Clausewitz criticized both Bülow and Jomini for their development of 'fantastic and one-sided systems'.[6] One of Clausewitz's last pieces of historical writing was an account of the 1796 French campaign against the Austrians in Italy, when the young Napoleon had revealed his incipient military genius. The campaign became the departure point for Jomini's own analysis of how Napoleon had changed the methods of war from those of his eighteenth-century predecessors. Clausewitz said of it, on the opening page of his own account, that Jomini's 'narrative is insufficient, full of gaps, obscure, contradictory – in short it is everything that an overall account of events and their relationships should not be'.[7]

In all probability Clausewitz had not even crossed Jomini's horizon until these words were published in 1833, two years after Clausewitz's death, but Jomini rose to the challenge. In 1838 the Preface to his *Précis de l'art de la guerre*, whose qualities as a textbook established a pattern for works on strategy which has persisted until today, stated that Clausewitz has 'an easy pen' (significantly the French word was *facile*). 'But this pen,' Jomini went on, 'sometimes a little wayward, is in particular too pretentious for a didactic discussion, where simplicity and clarity must be the first requirement. More than that, the author reveals himself to be too sceptical in relation to military science: his first volume is only a blast against every theory of war, while the two following volumes, full of theoretical maxims, prove that the author believes in the efficacy of his own doctrines, even if he does not believe in those of others. As for me, I aver that I have been able to find in this labyrinthine intellect only a few insights and noteworthy points; and far from having caused me to share the author's scepticism, no work has contributed more than his to make me aware of the necessity and usefulness of good theories.'[8]

Jomini's criticisms of Clausewitz are worth quoting at length, precisely because they have never been wholly dismissed. Between 1834, when the last of the three volumes of *On War* was published, and 1871, Clausewitz was little read outside his native Prussia. Partly this was a consequence of his having written in German, a less accessible language to the literati of Europe than French. A Belgian artillery officer, Neuens, translated *On War* into French in 1849–51, and La Barre Duparcq, an instructor at St Cyr, France's military academy, then wrote a commentary on the text in 1853. Duparcq's reactions mirrored those of Jomini. He thought *On War* contained many insights but peddled false judgements and lacked overall clarity. For Clausewitz's fellow Prussians there were plenty of other works to read, even if none matched the ambition of his conception. When the publishers of *On War* somewhat optimistically decided to bring out a second and revised edition in 1853, the first printing of 1,500 copies had still not sold out. In 1857, a famous military commentator of the day, Wilhelm Rüstow, while comparing Clausewitz to Thucydides and saying he was 'good for all times', confessed that he 'has become well known, but is very little read'.[9]

Like Jomini's judgement, Rüstow's has never lost its force. However, Prussia's stunning and rapid victories over Austria in 1866 and France in 1870–71, culminating in the unification of Germany, inaugurated the first true discovery of Clausewitz. The German army now became the model for Europe, and Clausewitz was cast as its intellectual father. *On War* was translated into English by J. J. Graham in 1873. Four more German editions of *On War* were published before the First World War, and the fifth, published in 1905, had a Foreword by the Chief of the General Staff, Alfred von Schlieffen. Six editions appeared during the war itself, together with a host of abridged versions and short guides.

It is not at all clear why this should have been the case. In his old age, the architect of Prussia's victories, Helmuth von Moltke, included *On War* in a small clutch of books which had influenced him, alongside more predictable titles such as the Bible and the works of Homer. It became axiomatic that Clausewitz was Moltke's spiritual father. But there is no evidence to suggest that their paths crossed when Moltke was at the War Academy in the 1820s; although Clausewitz was its director, he did not teach. As Chief of the General Staff, Moltke trained his officers through practical exercises like staff rides and war games, not through works of theory. Certainly, if Moltke took anything from *On War*, it was not the precepts on war's relationship to policy or its 'trinitarian' nature in the terms which they came to be understood by Colin Powell or Martin van Creveld. Famously, Moltke rebutted the efforts of Prussia's Minister President (and Germany's first Chancellor), Otto von Bismarck, to assert the primacy of policy during the course of the Franco–Prussian war, claiming that policy's influence was decisive only at the opening and at the end of a conflict. 'Strategy has no choice but to strive for the highest goal attainable with the means given,' he said in 1871. 'The best way in which strategy can cooperate with diplomacy is by working solely for political ends but doing so with complete independence of action.'[10] Prussia achieved a crushing victory over Napoleon III at Sedan on 1 September 1870 but the war was prolonged until 10 May 1871. With the fall of Napoleon, the Third Republic resolved to wage a war of national resistance. Moltke's response to this intervention by the people was not to recognize the war's 'trinitarian' nature but to do his best to deny it – to say that France's guerrillas flouted the laws of war and to affirm that in Germany's own case the army, although it was conscripted, should embrace an ethos that derived not from the people but from the monarchy and its officer corps.

Gerhard Ritter, the great historian of German militarism, concluded that Moltke's conceptions, 'despite the fact that they deliberately hark back to certain formulations by Carl von Clausewitz... represent a clear departure from Clausewitz's basic views'. During the siege of Paris, in the winter of 1870–71, when the clash between Bismarck and Moltke reached its height, Moltke declared 'political elements merit consideration only to the extent that they do not make demands that are militarily improper or impossible'.[11] This was an opinion that was indeed incompatible with the parts of On War on which Ritter and subsequent commentators have focused – that is the first and last of its eight books, and in particular the first book's first chapter. It is here that the most cogent expression of war's relationship to policy is to be found, and it is this chapter which concludes with the 'trinity'. Moltke and his contemporaries read the intervening books of On War just as – if not more – carefully, precisely because they described the Napoleonic wars whose paradigm (not least thanks to Jomini) dominated military thought until 1914. The wars of German unification were short, sharp and decisive. That was both a Napoleonic and a Clausewitzian ideal. Battle settled strategy. What Moltke and his immediate successors understood by strategy was exclusively military, somewhat closer to today's usage of 'the operational level of war'. It was here that the key debates about military theory took place between 1871 and 1914. Strategy was what generals and their staffs did (and they, after all, were the most likely readers of a big book on war); it underpinned manoeuvres and exercises; and it guided the plans with which they embarked on hostilities in 1914 itself. In 1866 and 1870 Moltke had achieved decisive success because his armies had converged on the battlefield from different directions, so taking his opponents in the flank and rear as well as from the front. Although Napoleon had done the same thing, not least in his early campaigns in Italy, Clausewitz did not endorse the use of what soldiers call envelopment. In this he and Jomini were at one, and the latter – still alive in 1866, if not in 1870 – criticized Prussia's conduct of the war with Austria for that very reason. Moltke engaged with *On War* because he engaged with, and decided to modify, classical strategy, not policy. Writing in 1871, Moltke concluded in one of the rare passages where he cited Clausewitz directly: 'General von Clausewitz... said "Strategy is the use of the engagement for the goal of the war". In fact, strategy affords tactics the means for fighting and the probability of winning by the direction of armies and their meeting at the place of combat. On the one hand, strategy appropriates the success of every engagement and builds upon it. The demands of strategy grow silent in the face of a tactical victory and adapt themselves to the newly created situation.'[12]

Moltke and his successors saw *On War* as a discussion as much of the relationship between tactics, or what armies do on the battlefield, and strategy, or the use of the results they achieve on the battlefield, as of that between war and policy. And they were not wrong. In particular, Clausewitz's attention to issues of morale and courage, of will and insight, seemed even more relevant in the tactical conditions of the late nineteenth century than they had been at its beginning. Industrialization had transformed the battlefield into a fire-swept zone, traversed by breech-loading rifles, machine guns and quick-firing artillery. It had also sucked populations out of the countryside into the big cities. There, the combination of slum-dwelling, vicious leisure pursuits and urban decadence seemed to be breeding people that were unfit, both physically and psychologically, for the rigours of war.

France's love affair with Clausewitz made these points even more obvious than did Germany's. As the defeated power after 1871, France had more cause to look at the sources of Germany's success than did Germany itself. In 1885 Lucien Cardot lectured on Clausewitz at the École de Guerre, and in 1886–7 Lieutenant Colonel de Vatry produced a fresh translation of *On War* but significantly only of Books 3 to 6, those most concerned with Napoleonic warfare and those in which Vatry himself reckoned strategic principles were most clearly enunciated. These were not the books of *On War* which so impressed Colin Powell or which underpinned Martin van Creveld's 'Clausewitzian universe'. Vatry did go on to translate the rest of *On War*, but significantly Clausewitz's best-known French interpreter of the period, Georges Gilbert, said that he need not have bothered. In 1890 Gilbert declared that Clausewitzian theory could be summarized in three laws: to act simultaneously with all forces concentrated; to act quickly and most often with a direct blow; and to act without pause.[13]

Among Cardot's and Gilbert's auditors at the École de Guerre was the man who in 1918 would command the combined French, British and American forces on the Western Front in the First World War, Ferdinand Foch. In a series of lectures delivered at the École de Guerre in 1901, Foch said that the defeat in 1871 had woken the French to the fact that the nature of war was to be understood through history, that this was the method that Clausewitz had used, and that 'in the book of History, carefully analysed', Clausewitz had found 'the living Army, troops in movement and action, with their human needs, passions, weaknesses, self-denials, capacities of all sorts'. Moral forces and will power were crucial to victory. However, because both sides aspired to superiority in these respects, the enemy 'will only consider himself beaten when he is no longer able to fight: that is, when his army shall have been materially and morally destroyed'. 'Therefore', Foch was able to conclude, 'modern war can only consider those arguments which lead to the destruction of that army: namely battle, overthrow by force.'[14] Clausewitz expressed himself in just such terms, as Foch himself demonstrated by direct quotation.

This was the Clausewitz to whom the British military commentator Basil Liddell Hart would take such strong exception after the First World War. During the war Foch put into practice what he preached, or at least he never specifically retracted it. Foch, Liddell Hart wrote in 1931 in a biography of the French marshal, 'had caught only Clausewitz's strident generalizations, and not his subtler undertones'. Thus Liddell Hart's Clausewitz was one mediated by the generals of the First World War. The implication in his criticism of Foch was that there was another Clausewitz. But if he really believed that, he never acted on it. In Liddell Hart's mind the guts of the problem lay not with Foch, but with Clausewitz himself: 'The ponderous tomes of Clausewitz are so solid as to cause mental indigestion to any student who swallows them without a long course of preparation. Only a mind developed by years of study and reflection can dissolve the solid lump into digestible particles.'[15] In his Lees Knowles lectures, delivered at Cambridge in 1932–3, Basil Liddell Hart blamed Clausewitz for the slaughter of the First World War, memorably but somewhat meaninglessly dubbing him 'the Mahdi of Mass'. He declared that, 'Clausewitz's principle of force without limit and without calculation of cost fits, and is only fit for, a hate-maddened mob. It is the negation of statesmanship – and of intelligent strategy, which seeks to serve the ends of policy.'[16]

If Liddell Hart had been right, there would have been no need for Martin van Creveld and others to have declared Clausewitz dead after the Cold War; he would already have been knocked from his pedestal after the First World War. Indeed, in France and Britain (where his perch had in any case been much rockier) he was. But that did not apply in his homeland.

Defeat in 1918 prompted Germans to return to Clausewitz, not to ditch him. This time round, however, they read him in different ways. The second discovery of Clausewitz was pioneered less by soldiers, as had been the case after 1871, than by academics. Before the First World War, Hans Delbrück, himself a veteran of the Franco–Prussian War and a professor in Berlin, had argued that, if Clausewitz had lived, he would have gone on to develop a system for strategy that would have recognized two different forms of waging war. The first would have been a strategy of annihilation. The second would have been a strategy designed to wear the enemy out, so that he would agree to negotiate. Delbrück had argued, somewhat tendentiously, that the king of Prussia, Frederick the Great, had tried to do the second of these in the Seven Years War between 1756 and 1763, an interpretation vigorously contested by the historians of the General Staff. In some respects, both sides were reflecting the preoccupations of their own callings. Delbrück was looking at strategy in a political context; Frederick sought a negotiated peace because Austria was confronted by an alliance of France, Russia and Prussia, and so was not strong enough to hope for more. The General Staff conceived of strategy in a military or operational light: for them Frederick sought battle, not shunned it, especially when it gave him the opportunity to deal with one of his enemies in isolation. The German army entered the First World War convinced that there was only one way to fight a war, and that way was the strategy of annihilation resulting in complete German victory: its operational thought was scaled up to the level of policy.

Delbrück maintained a running commentary on the war

as it unfolded and after it was over renewed his attacks on the army's approach to strategy – and especially on Erich Ludendorff, the de facto head of the German army between 1916 and 1918. What Delbrück's extrapolations from *On War* brought out was the role of dialectics in Clausewitzian thought. Books 3 to 5 of *On War*, those on which many military theorists of 1871 to 1914 had concentrated, described a unitary conception of war, predominantly derived from the Napoleonic wars and concerned with strategy in an operational sense; both the beginning of *On War*, Books 1 and 2, and the end, Books 6, 7 and 8, allowed for alternatives. Even as the First World War ended, a youthful German scholar, Hans Rothfels, was putting the finishing touches to his doctoral thesis on Clausewitz's early career and its role in the formulation of his ideas. The parallel seemed direct. In 1806, Prussia was defeated by France. Clausewitz had found himself in the same position as many young Germans in 1918. His own life and times therefore became important to the interpretation of his work. *On War* was not to be read as a staff college manual, in bits, but as a whole, and it was to be seen in the context of the philosophical ideas which underpinned it. At the operational level, this involved the rediscovery of Book 6, with its declaration that the defence was stronger than the offence, a precept with particular resonance for those who had fought in the trenches in 1914–18, and who also found fresh merit in Clausewitz's description of battle as a form of attrition. But the most important consequence of this spate of activity, and particularly of Rothfels's own work, was the reconsideration of what Clausewitz had said about the relationship between war and policy.

The German army convinced itself that it had not lost the First World War, but that in November 1918 revolution at home had precipitated defeat. The so-called 'stab in the back' led it to pay more attention to the third element of Clausewitz's 'trinity', the people. Ludendorff recognized that war now involved the full mobilization of the entire resources of the nation. In a book published in 1922, *Kriegführung und Politik*, Ludendorff began with a respectful discussion of Clausewitz's ideas, which said (not quite accurately) that for Clausewitz policy meant only foreign policy, not domestic policy, but that the First World War, which for Germany was a war for existence, showed that references to policy in *On War* should now be understood to apply to both. Moreover, as his title made clear, the conduct of war, *Kriegführung*, should be put ahead of policy: the latter should serve the former, and not vice versa. In *Der totale Krieg*, which appeared in 1935, he went further. The proper translation of this title is not 'total war', but, as the English edition (which is called *The Nation at War*) makes clear, 'totalitarian war'. Ludendorff's attention was not on how to wage war against an enemy in the operational sense, but on how to mobilize the whole state for war. 'All the theories of Clausewitz should be thrown overboard,' he wrote. 'Both warfare and politics are meant to serve the preservation of the people, but warfare is the highest expression of the national "will to live", and politics must, therefore, be subservient to the conduct of war.'[17]

Ironically, therefore, Ludendorff joined Liddell Hart in blaming the conduct of the First World War on Clausewitz. For Ludendorff, the problem was that the First World War was so different from earlier wars that *On War* had saddled Germany with a conception of war's nature that was too limited. Liddell Hart on the one hand wanted to demolish Clausewitz because he wanted to restrict war; Ludendorff on the other wanted to abandon him because he wanted to widen the scope of policy: 'like the totalitarian war, politics, too, must assume a totalitarian character'.[18] Ludendorff therefore acted as a bridge between the ideas of the German General Staff in 1914–18 and the rhetoric of Fascism. By eroding the distinctions between war and peace, and defining politics as an existential struggle for survival, the Nazis imported the vocabulary of war to daily life. But, contrary to Ludendorff's beliefs, totalitarianism did not imply the death of Clausewitz. Karl Haushofer, the professor of geopolitics at Munich and himself a National Socialist, delivered a copy of *On War* to the political prisoners held in Landsberg prison after the failed Nazi *Putsch* of 1924. In 1933, as the Nazis seized power, he wrote to one of them, Rudolf Hess, 'Remember the word of Clausewitz, so that you yourself can rouse the German nation to life again.'[19] The Clausewitz who appealed to the Nazis was less the theorist of war whom Ludendorff rejected and more the spokesman of an existential conflict with Napoleonic France, whom the academics had discovered but Ludendorff had overlooked. 'Not all of you may have read Clausewitz, and, if you have read it you have not understood it and realized how to apply it to the future,' Adolf Hitler told an audience in Munich on 9 November 1934. 'Clausewitz writes that recovery is still always possible after a heroic collapse... It is always better, indeed necessary, to embrace an end with horror than to suffer horror without end.'[20]

In April 1945, less than nine years later, these words would acquire an awful reality for the German nation as the Red Army closed on Berlin. Hitler did indeed embrace 'an end with horror' in a battle which represented the clash of two contrasting interpretations of Clausewitz's thinking on the relationship between war and policy. *On War* was not translated into Russian until 1902, and inadequately even then. But a fresh version appeared in 1932–3, and it had reached its fifth Russian edition by the time of the German invasion of Russia in 1941. The appeal of Clausewitz to totalitarian governments was therefore confirmed by his reception in the Soviet Union. In 1858 the founding father of Communism, Karl Marx, had written of Clausewitz, that 'the fellow has a common sense that borders on wit'.[21] The Bolshevik party leader, V. I. Lenin, was particularly taken by Clausewitz's formulation that war was waged for the ends of policy and made extensive use of *On War* when he wrote his essay on socialism and war while in exile in Switzerland in 1915. After the Russian Revolutions of 1917, Lenin's chief executive, Leon Trotsky, tried to balance the political imperatives of revolutionary socialism with military realities as he set about the creation of the Red Army. For him, the dialectical approach of Books 1 and 8 held a particular appeal: 'We must reject all attempts at building an absolute revolutionary strategy with the elements of our limited experience of three years of civil war during which army sections of a special quality engaged in combat under special conditions. Clausewitz has warned very correctly against this.'[22]

The symmetry between Marxism–Leninism and Clausewitz was challenged by the bitter fighting of the Russo–German war of 1941–5. By 1945 Clausewitz laboured under three besetting sins in Russian eyes: first, he was German, and therefore his ideas were those of the enemy; second, German military thought had been responsible for two world wars; and third, the German way of war had proved remarkably unsuccessful in both, resulting in successive and resounding defeats. The problem of Lenin's enthusiasm for *On War* was dealt with by explaining that he never addressed the specifically military side of Clausewitz's thinking. What appealed to Lenin was the observation that war was a continuation of policy, but that attracted him because he was a Marxist, and Clausewitz, self-evidently, was not. In February 1946, the party leader, Josef Stalin, declared that Clausewitz was out of date, 'a representative of the age of manufactures in war', whereas 'now we stand in the machine age of war'.[23]

reached conclusions set by geometry, not rooted in war as he had experienced it. The purpose of Books 2 to 6 of *On War*, therefore, was to deal with war as it really was, precisely to develop sound principles. These books are distinguished less by debate than by the establishment of their own precepts: they are the ones which convey a unitary image of war. In Book 3 (on strategy), chapter 14, Clausewitz wrote: 'Soon the actor in war must simplify the law to some prominent characteristic points which form his rules, soon the method which he has adopted must become the staff on which he leans.'[23] Moreover, many of the principles which Clausewitz endorsed are to be found in Jomini as well.

Clausewitz magnified his differences with Jomini, Bülow and others for a purpose. He did not cite military writers of his own day with whom he agreed. Mention has already been made of Guibert. Equally noteworthy for their absence are the Germans, Georg Heinrich von Berenhorst, whose *Betrachtungen über den Kriegskunst* (1797) anticipated Clausewitz in several ways, not least in his emphasis on moral and psychological factors in war, and Johann Jakob Otto August Rühle von Lilienstern, Clausewitz's direct contemporary, who had stressed that war fulfilled political purposes in his war school lectures, published as a handbook for officers in 1817–18. Their omission may be due to vanity, to Clausewitz's own intellectual arrogance. But it also reflects their redundance in Clausewitz's scheme of things: his argument did not need them, even as buttresses for his more controversial assertions, but it did need Jomini and Bülow. They were the fall guys off whom he could bounce his propositions. Much of *On War* is a dialogue. In this Clausewitz is different from many other writers on strategy, not least Jomini, who tend to present conclusions rather than engage in argument and debate. But Clausewitz's predilection for the dialectical method is much less evident in Books 2 to 5, those in which he is describing late Napoleonic warfare and spelling out the principles to be derived from it, than it is in Books 1 and 8, those which have had a much more lasting influence on strategic thought.

Again, the completion of Book 6 marks the change in approach. Book 6, which stresses that the defence is the stronger form of war with the negative aim, is in tension with Book 7, the attack, which is the weaker form of war with the positive aim. Therefore, one of Clausewitz's central themes, that war is a reciprocal activity which depends on the clash of forces to occur at all, has become an analytical method. The big challenge that confronted him, as he embraced both the dialectic of attack and defence within war and the dialectic within his own book, was what that meant for his yen to find a system. The note of 1827 deepened the dilemma, with its statement that there were two sorts of wars. As the influence of dialectics became progressively stronger in Book 8, it confronted him with fresh challenges. One was the consequence of his own dialogue between theory and reality. It is not always clear from his writings when Clausewitz is establishing a normative principle as opposed to reflecting on experience. This is a natural outgrowth of his approach to principles, which he sees not as invariably true, but as generally true in the majority of cases – and that is precisely their value.

By December 1827 policy had become the basis for a new synthesis. Methodologically Clausewitz moved on from dialectics – from the Socratic mode of enquiry, which by leaving no assumption unchallenged was in danger of destroying more than creating – to a greater positivism. Throughout *On War*, Clausewitz displayed a propensity for seeing issues in threes. Many of these trios were prosaic. There were three reasons for having stronger vanguards in the centre, three conditions affecting the establishment of camps, three conditions under which armies could be quartered, three spatially distinct bases of operations, three effects of terrain on war, three types of pursuit, three strategic assets in controlling high ground, three factors which gave the decisive advantage in an engagement (surprise, the benefit of the terrain and concentric attack), and three advantages in mounting a converging attack.[24] So great was the drive to create groups of three, greater than logic alone suggested, that they could be the consequence of contrivance. Clausewitz said that there were three sorts of terrain different from plains; they were mountains, forests and marshes, and agricultural areas.[25] But what was the logic that lumped forests and marshes into a single category, when their impact on fighting could clearly be very different? And why were not plains themselves deemed to be a fourth type of terrain? In this case five categories were lurking under Clausewitz's rule of three.

Clausewitz's use of threes was repeated and frequent, although rarely as doggedly adhered to as in this case. It developed from being a device for enumerating issues on which he wished to comment, or distinctions which he wished to draw, to being a means for defining concepts central to his understanding of war. Victory was evident in three ways – in the enemy's loss of material strength, in the blow to his morale, and in his decision to abandon his intentions; the outcome of battle was measured by its psychological effect in the opposing general, the casualties that his army suffered, and the ground that he gave up; and its effects were therefore felt on the commanders, on the belligerent states, and on the course of the war.[26] What is evident here is that the groups of three combine to form a whole. Many of the pairs created by Clausewitz's dialectics gain by the injection of a third component. The third element, although possibly complicating the analysis, gives it depth. Thinkers on the conduct of war tend to pair time and space, and assess the trade-off in their interaction. Clausewitz does so too, but he also injects manpower. Moreover, space, masses and time are expressed in the theatre of war, the army and the campaign itself.[27]

Clausewitz's distinction between the military aim within the war and the political purpose of the war as a whole is a classic illustration of the dialectic process in operation: in so far as policy impinges on Books 2 to 5 (and it does not very much), the two are in tension. But both – Clausewitz points out – have to take into account a third element, the means available, which is largely set by the government (in other words, policy in action) and not by the general. In his 1804 writings, Clausewitz talked about elementary tactics and higher tactics, the first the sort of combat which small units do and the second that of larger formations. He also talked about something on a larger scale again which he called operations (although whether he meant the operational level of war as it is now understood is a subject to which we shall return in the next chapter). Policy was therefore a fourth or possibly fifth level to war. But in *On War*, Clausewitz is concerned primarily with tactics and strategy, both as single entities, and the interaction between them. When policy is included, it therefore becomes the third element. As the letters to Roeder of December 1827 make clear, policy became the means not just for developing an idea but for harmonizing it – so seeing its unity. The notion of the trinity, of three in one, so clearly stated at the end of Book 1, chapter 1, and which will be discussed in Chapter 4 of this book, therefore has a long pedigree in Clausewitz's thinking.

This polarity – between war as instrumental, controllable by human agency, and war as beyond human controls – is mirrored in Clausewitz's varied use of law as a metaphor for war. Law as practised by lawyers in litigation was not only the product of reciprocal activity between two sides, as war is, but also a set of general rules subject to modification in practice. The analogy between this sort of law and the principles of war also worked in one of the two ways in which Clausewitz used the laws of mathematics. The laws of probability played to Clausewitz's desire to systematize, to establish what is generally true or what might normally be expected to happen. But Clausewitz also used law in a more fixed, unalterable and elemental sense, as when we speak of the laws of nature. Here he was the pupil of Isaac Newton, falling back on his readings in physics and the mechanical sciences, to produce concepts central to his thinking on war, including those of the centre of gravity, of equilibrium, and of friction. These will all be discussed in subsequent chapters, but the point here is that they were intrinsic to war itself and beyond manipulation by human agency.

Even more overt in Clausewitz's methods than his reliance on law or science is his use of philosophy. He repeatedly employed the word 'philosophical' to describe his way of thinking through the problems that he was addressing.[28] But, as with his debt to military theorists, he was sparing in specific acknowledgement of those who inspired him. His 1804 notes show that he had by then already read Niccolò Machiavelli's *Discourses* (begun in 1513). Clausewitz admired Machiavelli's emphasis on the realities of power, presumably learning from him that war has a political purpose, and that war or the threat of war is ever present in the conduct of foreign policy. Clausewitz, like Machiavelli, treated war as outside moral categories, as a necessary part of governmental activity. However, the only political philosopher mentioned specifically in relation to *On War* was a figure not of the Renaissance but of the eighteenth-century French Enlightenment, Charles Louis de Secondat Montesquieu, and then only in an introductory note written around 1818. Clausewitz said that he aspired to the method of Montesquieu's *De l'esprit des lois* (1748) – 'precise, aphoristic chapters', which would attract the intelligent reader 'by what they suggested as much as by what they expressed'.[29] He achieved this in some of his early writing and again in Book 1, chapter 1. Montesquieu based his principles on the essential nature of the things he was describing. At one level, not least in its attention to the relationship between war and policy, but also in its exploration of the relationships between the different components of war, *On War* belongs in the tradition of the Enlightenment, and is indeed the culmination of its influence on military thought. Clausewitz tells us – through Marie – that it was as a result of his exposure to the work of the *philosophes* that he began the process of intellectual and spiritual awakening in the second half of the 1790s.

But by then Germany, not least in reaction to the dominance of the French language (a subject on which Clausewitz expressed himself forcefully on more than one occasion), found its own philosophical voice. Through his years in Berlin, 1801–6, 1808–11, and finally 1819–30, Clausewitz frequented exactly those circles where the ideas of the German Enlightenment, the *Aufklärung*, and its outgrowth, the *Sturm und Drang* movement, with its pointers away from rationality towards Romanticism, were current. Again, however, the connections between German philosophy and *On War* are more often expressed indirectly than directly.

The most obvious link is with Immanuel Kant. Johann Gottfried Kiesewetter, who wrote an outline of Kantian philosophy, taught mathematics and logic at the war school when Clausewitz was a pupil. It is hard to see Clausewitz as a Kantian in content: *On War* is grounded in reality and sees peace as the result of war; Kant's *Perpetual Peace* (1795) aspires to an ideal and sees peace as a moral aim. But what Clausewitz did learn from Kant was that there were two forms of truth. Formal truth united proposals with the laws of thought, and used logic to produce abstractions, which falsified reality through selection to produce an insight. Material truth united such insights with their counterparts, in the dialectical process so evident in some parts of *On War*. Clausewitz wrestled with this tension between concept and reality, seeking to reconcile them but also being aware of the distinction.[30]

Kant was over half a century older than Clausewitz. G. W. F. Hegel was only ten years his senior and died in the same year, also of cholera: the two frequented the same social circles in Berlin in the 1820s. In form and method Clausewitz may have been Kantian, but in substance he became progressively more Hegelian. Hegel's thought moved in step with the events of his times, as did Clause-witz's. In 1812, war for Hegel was an existential issue as it was for Clausewitz. But by 1827, Hegel concluded that war is fought not by individuals but by persons acting in their public capacities, as members of states. It is hard to distance this observation from Clausewitz's own contem-poraneous insight on war's relationship to policy. Both men progressively incorporated other forms of conflict than those which dominated their thoughts in 1806 and 1812. Like the later Clausewitz, Hegel was interested in the relations between the abstract and the concrete, and used dialectics to explore them, even if in Hegel's case the poles in the argument excluded each other, and could only be reconciled by idealism, whereas in Clausewitz's case they tend to depend on each other. By 1827 they both realized that the conduct of war needed to reflect the fact that its object was peace and that war's purpose should be seen not as existential, but instrumental.[31]

In the fevered atmosphere of the Napoleonic wars, Hegel identified with the state, as Clausewitz did. Hegel saw it as both embodying and enabling social freedom, and argued that the individual best demonstrated his absolute freedom by putting his life at risk. Both were in contact with a third philosopher, Johann Gottlieb Fichte, who in 1814 succumbed to a fever contracted while serving with the Landsturm (a form of home guard) in the war of national liberation. Fichte's *Reden an die deutsche Nation* (1808) embodied the existential view of war in its most high-flown form: those who die in battle for freedom do not end life but give birth to freedom. Clausewitz read it when it appeared and approved of much of it, but found it too abstract and too distant from history and the world of experience.[32] None the less he responded in the following year to an article which Fichte had written on Machiavelli, and expressed himself in terms which harmonized the military reform movement with the philosophical currents to which not only Fichte but also Hegel were giving vent: 'The modern art of war, far from using men like simple machines, should vitalize individual energies as far as the nature of its weapons permits.'[33]

Clausewitz put his argument in the context of what he called 'the true spirit of war'. Montesquieu had talked of the spirit of the law, of institutions and of people; Hegel wrote of the phenomenonology of the spirit. The word 'spirit' is an important one, but – particularly in German – ambiguous. '*Geist*' can mean mind as well as inspiration; it can shade from the spiritual to the intellectual. In his 1804 notes Clausewitz used the word '*Intelligenz*' when he wished to describe the commander's rational processes, but he was at pains to say that the general did not need to be a learned person. A schoolmaster or a master-builder required far more learning; a commander needed 'very little knowledge and much exercise of judgement, very few abstract truths and many perspectives linked to the inner spirit'.[34] The early Clausewitz used *Geist* predominantly for abstractions – the spirit of the art of war, the spirit of the practice of war – but in this passage he anticipates its application in *On War*. He makes it a personal quality, a mark of character.

Clausewitz was therefore as much a Romantic as he was a child of the Enlightenment. The individual, as Hegel and Fichte also argued in relation to the state, was what gave life and meaning to the 'system' of war. Personality was not peripheral to the theory of war, but central; the same went for morale and its psychological effects. During his internment in France in 1807, Clausewitz met August Wilhelm Schlegel, who introduced him to the mystical current in Romanticism. His response to seeing Mont Blanc was the classic discovery of the Romantic: 'It is impossible to let the eyes wander with giant strides over the peaks of the rock walls, many thousands of feet high, without feeling the chest swell, the sense of potential rise and the soul fill with resolve and hope.'[35] These were the sentiments which enabled Clausewitz to tackle the tribulations of the years between Jena and Waterloo; this was the Clausewitz who told the Crown Prince in 1812 of 'the will, which in strong men dominates like an absolute ruler', and went on 'just as the light is concentrated at the centre of a fire, so the will unites the power of individuals,... bending nations before it and its awesomeness stripping the sages of their reason'.[36]

Clausewitz did not become a mystic, and the author of *On War* is more rational than the warrior of 1812. But he now largely abandoned the word '*Intelligenz*',[37] and instead

used 'Geist' almost exclusively when discussing the attributes of the commander. How 'Geist' is read is therefore
almost as crucial to the understanding of the book as is the
issue of the note of 1827. Peter Paret and Michael Howard
more often than not render it as 'intellect' or 'mind', rather
than 'spirit'. In doing so, they reflect one aspect of the
German word, but they also privilege the Enlightened
Clausewitz over the Romantic. Too much can be made of
the polarity, not enough of the evolution from one to the
other. 'Geist' clearly incorporates a rational element,
because the audacity of the commander has to be rooted in
good judgement. It is significant that what Clausewitz ultimately settles on is the idea of genius, the quality that sees
through the confusion of war to its core and then takes
decisive action.

Kant, in his theory of art, had dispensed with the
Enlightenment's belief that genius should be set in the
context of rules, and had seen it as the sole source of artistic
creativity. Clausewitz, his artistic awareness given life by
Marie and his sojourn in France, wrote an essay on art and
the theory of art. Many of his explorations of other fields of
human endeavour gave him only the metaphors which
became such powerful ways of elucidating his ideas
through analogy, but in this case the effect was more perva-
sive. Following Kant, he argued that the artistic genius
does not break the rules but works within them; the truly
great artist may rewrite the rules, but then the rules themselves change, and so the dialogue between genius and

rules persists. Clausewitz applied these insights from the fine arts to the art of war.[38] Napoleon was a genius, who himself embodied the *Geist* of the art of war, and the challenge for Clausewitz was to find the rules which reflected the consequences of his actions. As he wrote to Fichte, 'begin not with the form but with the spirit, in the certain anticipation that this itself will break the old forms and will result in forms that are better adapted'.[39]

The title of Book 2 of *On War* is 'the theory of war'. Clausewitz aspired to write a theory of war that was not only new but also – thanks to the rigour of his analysis – usable. 'Part of the object of this book', he wrote, 'is to determine whether a conflict of living forces as it develops and is resolved in war remains subject to general laws.'[40] Like his contemporaries, he began, therefore, not with history, but with theory. His notes from 1804 are statements of theory with occasional historical references, and his serious historical output did not precede, but followed, his decision in 1816 to write a book on the theory of war. His initial inspiration came not from military history, but from his exposure to philosophy and, even more, from the fact that his own experiences of war did not match the theories that he had read. The primacy of philosophy remained fundamental to the disciplinary method which he applied to military theory and military history, and it provided the intellectual framework for an approach to theory which used reason to put the experiences of reality in order and thus to create new but verifiable propositions.

Clausewitz made clear that by theory he did not mean preparations for war or features ancillary to war. The theory of war was concerned with the use of war. Its purpose was to distinguish the different elements that make up war, and so to simplify and distil knowledge. Its essence therefore lay in study itself, exerting its influence on practical life more 'through critical analysis than through doctrine'.[41] That process, using theory as an aid to judgement, was what educated the commander. This did not mean, however, that the insights which theory vouchsafed should not be followed through to enable the establishment of principles, where that was logically viable. 'Principles, rules, regulations, and methods are... indispensable concepts to or for that part of the theory of war that leads to positive doctrines; for in these doctrines the truth can express itself only in such compressed forms.'[42] This was more likely to happen at the lower, tactical levels of war, where genius had less play, but Clausewitz did not rule it out in strategy if 'the arch of truth culminates in such a keystone... the point where all lines converge'. Principles derived from theory became vicious only when they became inflexible, when they ceased to be guides to thought and developed into prescriptive rules.[43] The commander had to know not only how to apply principles but also when to override them.

The strength of theory lay in insights rather than formulas, but its value was still rooted in its desire to generalize. In disciplines like philosophy this abstraction could be an end in itself. Clausewitz himself said that 'only a theory that will follow the simple thread of internal cohesion as we have tried to make ours do, can get back to the essence of things'.[44] But what he meant by that was the cohesion provided by the true nature of war, not by the demands of theory. The test of theory was reality, not abstract thought.[45] Clausewitz's principal reality check was his own experience, not, at least in the first instance, military history. 'Why is history so lacking in useful examples?', he querulously enquired in 1804.[46] Scharnhorst soon disabused him of this youthful cynicism, without – as his persistent side-swipes in *On War* testify – ever entirely removing it. 'The aim of historians rarely is to present the absolute truth,' he told the Crown Prince in 1812: 'they invent history instead of writing it'.[47] But he still told his young charge to read military history. War was too messy a business to permit theoretical concepts to be put fully into practice. Military history was the basis of theory and therefore its reference point. However, history, like theory itself, provided not formulas but exercises in judgement. In the final chapter of Book 2, Clausewitz concluded that historical examples could be used in four ways: to explain an idea; to demonstrate the application of an idea; to support a statement and so show that a phenomenon was possible; and to give a detailed account of a historical event in order to deduce a doctrine.

The challenge that confronted the Prussian soldiers of Scharnhorst's and Clausewitz's generation was precisely the consequence of this interaction between history and theory. The historical example of Frederick the Great had been made the basis for theory, but had then prevented the Prussian army understanding subsequent changes in the conduct of war and had led directly to the disaster at Jena. Theory, therefore, could not be based on a single example. Those 'who would construct all history of individual cases – starting always with the most striking feature, and digging only as deep as it suits them, never get down to the general facts that govern the matter'.[48]

This was what Clausewitz did not like about history, that it was built up from individual cases. He particularly disliked the phrase that there was an exception to every rule.[49] 'No matter how it is constituted,' Clausewitz wrote at the beginning of Book 2, 'the concept of fighting remains unchanged.'[50] By the end of his work on *On War*, he had become clear that whatever else he achieved it must rise above the particular and circumstantial. In Book 8, chapter 3, he surveyed the history of war, acknowledging changes in its forms over time, but concluding that something much more general – Clausewitz used the word *ganz*, meaning 'whole' and 'entire' – had to be the aim of theory.

This was not the limit of history's deficiencies. Although using history as a critic and theorist rather than as a historian, Clausewitz was sufficiently historically minded to be aware of the difficulties which sources pose for historians. Equipped with hindsight, they could see things much more clearly than could the commander on the ground, and those who were not practitioners fell back on empty phrases which sounded expert but conveyed little. Reading a general's memoirs was not likely to be much more helpful, because they tended to be selective and self-serving. Detailed and careful analyses of the sources were the corrective for these tendencies, but that requirement in turn limited the chronological range that Clausewitz could exploit.[51]

For much of the eighteenth century, military writers had cited the works of classical authors. In some instances the references to Xenophon or Caesar were just form; in others, particularly in the debate on infantry tactics as to the merits of column over line, examples from ancient history were integral to the debate. Although Clausewitz referred to Hannibal and Caesar in his 1804 notes, by the time he came to write *On War* he concluded that illustrations from the ancient world were useless. This rejection of classical precepts, in itself a breach with the intellectual methods of the Enlightenment, was prompted not only by the power and relevance of more recent examples but also by quite proper historical considerations. The problems of sources were more acute the further back in time one went. Clausewitz went on to say that only conflicts since the war of Austrian succession, which began in 1740, were sufficiently close to the conditions of the modern day. But he was certainly much less dogmatic on this point than he was on the need to recognize the weight of apparently minor elements and details, now no longer retrievable but possibly of considerable significance to the outcome. He was far better versed in the history of seventeenth-century warfare than a superficial reading of *On War* sometimes suggests. In Book 5, he took the period between the Thirty Years War and the wars of Louis XIV, and specifically the War of the Spanish Succession (1701–14), as the departure point for modern war, saying that the conclusion to the first of those conflicts, the Peace of Westphalia of 1648, marked the initiation of more recent wars. Moreover, he saw Gustavus Adophus, the king of Sweden who was killed at the battle of Lützen in 1632, as the first of 'three Alexanders' who foreshadowed Napoleon. One calculation is that Clausewitz had studied over 130 campaigns.[52]

However, there were two further constraints on the span of military history which the theorist might properly exploit. The first was practical. The emphasis on detail and the suggestion that the era of modern war could bridge a couple of centuries created the problem not of too few sources, but of too many. Theory provided a short cut, 'so one need not start afresh each time sorting out the material and ploughing through it', and this precept applied to the student as much as to the practitioner: 'we must admit that wherever it would be too laborious to determine the facts of the situation, we must have recourse to the relevant principles established by theory'.[53]

The second was the product of the dramatic change in the conduct of war wrought by the French Revolution and Napoleon. Jomini had tried to integrate the wars of the

French Revolution with those of Fredrick the Great, a process made easier by the fact that Jomini began his major study before Austerlitz was fought in 1805, and so was using early Napoleonic warfare, not the later campaigns, as his yardstick. By the time he came to the writing of Book 8, Clausewitz was clear that that was a waste of effort. This did not mean, as some critics have implied, that *On War* is focused solely on warfare after 1806, to the exclusion of the wars of the French Revolution. Clausewitz wrote his histories of the 1796 and 1799 campaigns at roughly the same time as Book 8. It is, however, a recurrent and even dominant theme of Book 8 that modern war, far from beginning in 1648 or 1740, as he had suggested in the earlier books of *On War*, actually began in 1792.

The apparent beauty of this conclusion for Clausewitz is that it seemed to open out the possibility of a reconciliation of the dialectic between theory and history. The gap between theory and practice for the Prussian army he had joined had been a consequence of the misapplication of history and had been stripped bare by the French on the battlefield in 1806. Theory was weaker, Clausewitz argued, where wars were fought for half-hearted objectives, and stronger when war was 'more obedient to the law of inner necessity'. Napoleonic war brought theory and practice into alignment. But just at the moment when this approach seemed to make synthesis possible, history reared its head once more. Clausewitz did not know the shape of future war, and therefore had no choice but to refer to the past for his models, and that made him unsure as to which form of war, the Napoleonic or the pre-Napoleonic, would recur. 'We admit, in short,' he concluded, 'that in this chapter we cannot formulate any principles, rules or methods: history does not provide a basis for them. On the contrary, at almost every turn one finds peculiar features that are often incomprehensible, and sometimes astonishingly odd.'[54]

The circular nature of Clausewitz's dialectical argument is in danger of hiding the fact that *On War* is also moving forward. That status can also be lost sight of not least when, confusingly, the opening chapter is said to be the most complete. This progression has direct consequences for Clausewitz's use of language. Clausewitz wrote in a German that favoured the passive tense, and that produced long sentences, with several dependent phrases. The scope for ambiguity that this created was compounded by his enthusiasm for words that carried several layers of meaning. *Geist* is one; *Politik*, as we shall see, is another. The challenge for any translation of *On War* is whether to be consistent, rendering the same word the same way, or whether to interpret it according to the context into which it falls. Howard and Paret opted for the latter, acquiring clarity as they did so, but occasionally at the price of accuracy and even of interpretation. Those who have preferred literalness at least have the virtue of reflecting Clausewitz's own aspirations. He appreciated the connections between theory and vocabulary, recognizing that 'in theoretical discussion, particular terms should be reserved for particular qualities'. He therefore aimed to use his work to define concepts as best he could 'to serve as an approach to greater clarity and precision of language'.[55]

A central example of how this continuous process of refinement in the use of language could operate, and could create confusion in a text that is unfinished, is the balance between ends and means, a dialectic present throughout the text and central to Books 1 and 8. In Book 1, chapter 1, this duo becomes a triad, as the ends are themselves divided into two: the military aim within the war, say the defeat of the enemy army, where the German word *Ziel*, is used, and the political objective or purpose of the war, for example, a lasting peace settlement, where the German is *Zweck*. The trinitarian aspects of this are self-evident: the military aim, *Ziel*, is the means, *Mittel*, to the political objective, *Zweck*. Moreover, it is applicable at all levels within war as well as of war: the aim (*Ziel*) of a skirmish is the means (*Mittel*) to serve the objectives of strategy (*Zweck*), and so on. Political scientists have made much of this distinction between *Ziel* and *Zweck*, pursuing it with a consistency that is not evident in the rest of *On War*. Apart from in Book 1, chapter 1, paragraph 11, Clausewitz uses the words as though they were interchangeable, and on occasion introduces entirely fresh synonyms for aim or objective, for example *Richtung* or *Absicht*. As early in the reader's progress as chapter 2 of the same book, specifically on purpose and means in war, the word that Clausewitz uses to describe the destruction of the enemy's armed forces, which following the preceding logic should be *Ziel*, or possibly – since it is a means to an end – *Mittel*, is *Zweck*. Elsewhere, even as late in the development of his argument as Books 7 and 8, *Ziel* is used of the peace itself. There are clearly moments throughout *On War* when the *Ziel/Zweck* distinction was important to Clausewitz, but this is a matter of interpretation and even subjective judgement. In Book 2, chapter 3, on whether war is an art or science, Clausewitz describes the *Zweck* of art and the *Ziel* of science – a difference which seems significant, especially in the light of the discussion in Book 1, chapter 1. But Howard and Paret in their translation gloss over the distinction entirely, and they may be justified if they are right in their assumption that Book 2, chapter 3, was written some years before the version which we have of Book 1, chapter 1, and was not revised after 1827. In Book 1, chapter 2, Howard and Paret translate *Ziel* as 'means', and then later on the same page as 'policy'. If Clausewitz had been consistent in his language, the word should be *Mittel* in the first instance and *Zweck* in the second; if Howard and Paret were being consistent with Clausewitz's own guidelines the translation should be 'aim' in both cases.[56]

The problems that the rendering of *On War* into English highlights are in some respects the problems of reading *On War* more generally. The cynic might conclude that, if Clausewitz had been vouchsafed eternal life, the book would still not be finished. That observation, at once trite but possibly true, is however more helpful than its glibness suggests. *On War*'s vitality rests in its spirit of enquiry. The fact that Clausewitz's thinking went through so many iterations is precisely what gives it strength and depth. The book is an intellectual exploration; its stimulus comes directly from the fact that it does not resolve all the issues that it raises into neat packages. Ultimately, however, the assumption which guided Michael Howard and Peter Paret in their translation was well founded: Clausewitz's mind, and especially his philosophical method, provide enough underlying unity and continuity for it to be right to treat the text as a whole, and so to acknowledge that the sum is greater even than the parts.

CHAPTER 3

The Nature of War

Two notes by Clausewitz make clear that his principal objective, at least until 1827, was not to discuss all aspects of war, but one in particular. The first, dated to 1818, states that he has addressed 'the major elements of so-called strategy', and the second, the undated note, describes the book as a manuscript on 'the theory of major war, strategy as it is called'.[1] Today the word 'strategy', used by governments to describe peacetime policies more than by armies to shape wars, has gained in breadth but has forfeited conceptual clarity. Clausewitz's definition of strategy was both narrower and more consistent: indeed it is here that *On War*'s claims to consistency principally reside. Strategy was 'the use of engagement for the object of the war'.[2] It embraced the triad of time, space and mass to decide where and when a battle would be fought and with what forces. Its focus was the conduct of a campaign within a theatre of war, not the overall purpose of the war, and it was therefore a matter for generals, not politicians. Nor was it concerned with actual combat, although that did not mean that strategy necessarily ceased to operate when the battle began. Strategy was what gave fighting significance; it exploited success on the battlefield and it created the conditions for the next battle, while victory itself was gained through combat and therefore was a matter of tactics.[3]

Clausewitz put the weight on strategy for two reasons. First, he thought it was what was most obviously new about modern war. Even a book as recent and as wide-ranging as Guibert's, published in 1772, used tactics, not strategy, in its title. In a paper written in December 1817, Clausewitz said that he found no trace of strategy in war until the reign of Louis XIV (1643–1715), and even then only in a rigid form.[4] In the end, *On War* traced strategy's roots back to Gustavus Adolphus in the Thirty Years War (1618–48). Gustavus Adolphus, like the generals of Louis XIV, had had to plan in order to be able to manoeuvre and fight. Since then, armies had become progressively bigger, with the result that the scope for strategy had expanded. In part, strategy was about scale; it was 'concerned with major bodies of troops, wide areas and substantial lengths of time'.[5] Secondly, strategy was the dominant and most important aspect of war as a whole.[6]

Tactics underpinned strategy. It is not quite true that the central books of *On War* have no dialectic. They concern the relationship between tactics and strategy, not the now much more famous dialectic of war and policy. Significantly Book 1, chapter 1, neither defines tactics and strategy nor addresses the interface between them. That itself is the clearest indication as to the importance of the 1827 note as a departure point in Clausewitz's thought. He had passed beyond the central theme of his writing up until 1827, the relationship between strategy and tactics, to take up a new one, that between strategy – or war more generally – and policy.

Ultimately Clausewitz would see war as made up of three elements, tactics, strategy and policy. In Book 2, chapter 2, he anticipated some elements of this discussion in a typical exploration of the relationship between ends and means, pointing out that the means of strategy is victory, that is tactical success, but it is strategy which gives the fight significance, while strategy is itself a means to the ultimate end of policy, which is peace. But the implications of this discussion were not made fully explicit until Book 8.[7] By contrast the relationship between tactics and strategy had preoccupied him since he was a young man. Tactics, he told Gneisenau in 1811, 'is the doctrine of the use of the armed forces in the engagement', whereas strategy, which is the essence of the art of war, 'is the use of trained armed forces for the objective of the war'.[8] The definitions in Book 2, chapter 1, of *On War* are virtually identical.

In Clausewitz's day many routine elements in the conduct of war linked strategy and tactics. Strategic manoeuvre only achieved its purposes through its tactical effects – either because it succeeded in bringing the enemy to battle or because the threat of combat induced another response. Advanced guards and outposts were on the cusp of strategy and tactics, as they detected where the enemy was, tried to divine his intentions, and then shaped the consequent engagement as the two sides converged: indeed, this shift from a strategic to a tactical function culminated in the likelihood of their being the first forces committed to combat. What in turn gave the battle meaning was the pursuit which followed the achievement of victory. Pursuit, and this was a point etched in Clausewitz's thinking by the Prussian experience in 1806, was where 'strategy… draws near to tactics in order to receive the completed assignment from it'.[9]

During the course of the twentieth century this overlapping relationship between strategy and tactics acquired a separate title of its own, that of operations. The operational level of war was placed between tactics and strategy, and became the focus for the development of doctrine in the United States after the Vietnam War; other NATO countries followed suit. Howard and Paret use the words 'operations' and 'operational' throughout their translation of *On War*, published in 1976. Clausewitz does not, and that seems to have been a conscious decision. In his 1804 notes he headed three paragraphs '*Operationsplan*', the 'planning of operations': his mention of the political objective is situated within this discussion. Yet in *On War* he eschews the word, often opting for something vague, like *Handeln*, which means 'business' or 'transaction', so stressing war's practical and everyday nature, and its place in human intercourse, or specifically *Krieg*, which means 'war'. The theatre of operations became the theatre of war, the plan of operations the plan of war. The reason for what to modern readers may appear a retrograde move in the evolution of military thought is that Clausewitz was clear that, although 'tactics and strategy are activities that permeate one another in time and space', they 'are none the less totally different'. The precise distinctions between the two might be unimportant in terms of the actual conduct of war, but they were vital to the development of theory. He saw operations, the buzz word of today's armies, as an obstacle to conceptual clarity.[10]

Book 6 of *On War*, on defence, clarified why the difference between strategy and tactics had to be maintained. In the last chapter of the preceding book, on military forces, in which he discussed the use of higher ground, Clausewitz had begun to explore the relationship between the strategic defence and the tactical offence and vice versa. Armies could fight defensively in strategic terms but offensively in tactical. The value of defensive positions, whether man-made, like fortifications or entrenchments, or geographical, like mountains or river lines, was defined by their tactical advantage. But such positions were also chosen for their strategic significance, because they commanded a major route or waterway, for example. From them the defenders might mount a purely passive tactical defence, but if they were successful they would need to exploit the results of their success by counter-attacking, an offensive action which itself could begin as tactical but might evolve into something strategic as its success grew and gave opportunities for exploitation. Ultimately what distinguished the strategic defence from the strategic offence in Clausewitz's mind was the status of the theatre of war: those defending their own territory were strategically on the defensive, however aggressive their conduct of the war within that area; those invading somebody else's territory were on the strategic offence, even if they turned over to the tactical defensive in order to hold what they had gained. This link between the theatre of war and national frontiers, first adumbrated in Book 6, was what pointed forward to the political determinants of war, and thus opened out the threefold nature of defence: tactical, strategic and political.[11]

It is in his discussion of defence that Clausewitz makes the difference between tactics and strategy explicit in the most sustained way. But it appears elsewhere. It is central to what he says about surprise, a standard principle of war in most military literature. Clausewitz regarded surprise as unimportant in strategy. A worsening diplomatic situation, preparations for the conduct of a campaign, and the geographical constraints on possible lines of advance all created warnings. Moreover, time and space were both extended in a strategic context and so undermined the opportunities for surprise which speed of movement might create. By the same token both were contracted on the battlefield and therefore tactical surprise was more easily achievable than strategic.

One way this could operate was through a second

principle central to Clausewitz's thought, that of the concentration of forces on the decisive point. However, he distinguished between the strategic and the tactical in its application. In strategy, all available forces should be massed in time and space, as 'the law of simultaneous use nearly always advances the main decision', that was to say the decisive battle. Holding back a strategic reserve, as the Prussians had done in 1806, was nonsensical, as the war could be lost in the first battle. But within the battle both time and space worked differently. A battle began with a wearing-out exchange of fire, designed to inflict casualties; the general's object should be to minimize losses in these early phases, husbanding his reserves until the point when the balance would swing, the crisis of the battle. 'The successive use of force in a tactical situation always postpones the main decision to the end of the battle.'[12] Therefore, a tactical reserve, as opposed to a strategic one, was vital. Clausewitz's examination of the allies' conduct of the Waterloo campaign both underpinned and widened these conclusions. In 1815 Wellington and Blücher had nearly delivered themselves into Napoleon's hands by dispersing too widely, allowing Napoleon to concentrate in time and space. Moreover, the Prussians had not conserved their manpower during the preceding battles at Ligny or Wavre, permitting their tactical reserves to be drawn into the firefight before either battle had reached its crisis. But at Waterloo they redeemed the situation, arriving on the battlefield late in the day, but at the crucial moment, using both surprise and reserves to maximum tactical effect.[13]

The Prussians' contribution to victory at Waterloo made a third point relevant to the distinction between strategy and tactics. 'In most cases', Clausewitz wrote, 'reinforcements are much more effective when approaching the enemy from flank and rear, just as a longer handle gives greater leverage.'[14] His image of battle itself, reflected in his accounts of three at which he had been present – Borodino, Ligny and Wavre – corroborates the notion that he is a theorist of 'old wars'. He described clashes between symmetrical forces, evenly matched and disciplined bodies of men, both bent on fighting each other, not between conventional forces and guerrillas, the latter evading combat and waging war among civilians. The prolonged fire-fight of the two opponents meant that 'the battle burnt for a long time with moderate efforts like damp powder'.[15] Fighting on parallel fronts in such circumstances wore down the other side but did not produce a decision; that depended on the tactical reserve, whose effect would be greatest if it struck the enemy in his flank or rear. 'The risk of having to fight on two fronts, and the even greater risk of finding one's retreat cut off, tend to paralyse movement and the ability to resist, and so affect the balance between victory and defeat.'[16]

At the strategic level, however, an army was less discomfited by having to fight on two fronts at once. Unlike an army in battle, it would not be arrayed in close order, but would be dispersed, articulated in divisions of (say) 10,000 men and even corps of (say) 30,000. By organizing the Grande Armée in corps, a formation of all arms, potentially as big as many armies in eighteenth-century battles, and capable of fighting an independent action for several hours, Napoleon fused strategic manoeuvre with decisive battle. In 1806 a French corps had pinned the main weight of the Prussian army at Auerstädt, permitting Napoleon to defeat the remainder at Jena, while in 1815 the French corps commander, Grouchy, had failed in a comparable mission at Wavre, ensuring Napoleon's defeat at Waterloo. For the French military theorist and historian of Napoleonic warfare, Hubert Camon, writing before the First World War, Clausewitz was a paradox: a soldier who had served in the Napoleonic wars, and who studied them deeply, yet failed to understand what Camon saw as the essence of Napoleonic warfare. Napoleon used manoeuvre, and especially his so-called *manoeuvre sur les derrières*, to ensure that he fought his battles on the best possible terms. One corps would grip the enemy from the front, while the remainder would swing to envelop him from his rear. The enemy would be forced to give battle to recover his lines of communication, but would do so on Napoleon's terms, not his own.

Clausewitz rejected the principle of strategic envelopment in favour of that of concentration. The corps system meant that part of an army could turn to face its flank and rear without the whole force forfeiting either overall unity those allowed for in Book 8. In the ninth section of the chapter Clausewitz seems to come to the somewhat pessimistic conclusion that the result of war is never final, thus allowing for the renewal of hostilities. In fact his point is at once both philosophical and more optimistic. He argued that the verdict of war was never in itself 'absolute', since the defeated state would regard it as transitory, but he suggested that therefore a long-term solution had to be found in the policies pursued subsequent to the peace. In the very next section, entitled 'the probabilities of real life take the place of the extreme and absolute demanded by theory', Clausewitz went on to say that 'in this way the whole field of war ceases to be subject to the strict law of forces pushed to the extreme'. Once the law of extremes in war, 'the intention of disarming the enemy and overthrowing him', lost sway, 'the political object of the war once more comes to the front'.[59] Clausewitz still allowed for wars of national existence in which policy would be less evident because it would be acting in harmony with war's true nature, which itself would more closely approach the ideal of absolute war. But the latter had now become an abstraction, and wars of national survival the exception, not the rule. If war were 'a complete, untrammelled, absolute manifestation of violence (as the pure concept would require), war would of its own independent will usurp the place of policy the moment policy had brought it into being; it would then drive policy out of office and rule by the laws of its own nature, very much like a mine that can explode only in the manner or direction predetermined by the setting'.[60] But Clausewitz did not now see war like that. War sprang from a political purpose and policy would remain the supreme consideration in its conduct: 'policy, therefore, will permeate the whole action of war and exercise continual influence upon it, as far as the nature of the explosive forces within it allow'.[61] In Book 1, Clausewitz argued that in real war policy permeates the entirety of its action, acting as a moderating influence, and – along with friction – preventing it from reaching its absolute ideal. But he had elided what he now felt policy should do to war with what policy actually does to war. In practice policy adapts to war, to its development and circumstances, as much as war adapts itself to policy. The dynamics of war, which Clausewitz had explained so graphically in earlier writings, could make the policy which had given rise to war inoperative, forcing the policy, not the war, to change direction. This was the function of strategy, which is precisely what the bulk of *On War* is about. In Book 1, chapter 1, Clausewitz the theorist had prevailed over Clausewitz's own experience, with the result that he presented norms as realities.

Book 1, chapter 1, embodied a rational and instrumental approach to war. But it also contained within it the seeds of an argument which both rescued Clausewitz from the tyranny of his own normative prescriptions and has helped explain Clausewitz's continuing importance for strategic thought since the end of the Cold War. In its eleventh section, entitled 'the political object now comes to the fore again', Clausewitz explained how the political purpose determined both the military objective and the scale of effort required to achieve that objective. The greater the predominance of the political purpose, the more – if that purpose was reduced – would the war also be reduced and the more evident would be its political purpose. But policy was not necessarily determinative: it was subject both to politics and, even more powerfully, to the nature of war itself. Amid all his rationalization, Clausewitz still acknowledged that war by its very nature possessed its own escalatory dynamic, what he had called 'the explosive forces within it'. These were more likely to be put into operation when the populations as a whole were involved: 'Between two peoples and states such tensions, such a mass of hostile feeling, may exist that a motive for war, very trifling in itself, still can produce a wholly disproportionate effect – a positive explosion.'[62]

Clausewitz introduced here a polarity between policy and passion, between government and people, which was developed and resolved in his best-known trinity. The very last section of Book 1, chapter 1, a mere half page on the consequences of what had gone before for theory, described war as a something that continually changes its characteristics. It consists of three dominating tendencies, which work in different and variable combinations in each concrete case – 'violence, hatred and enmity, which are to be regarded as blind natural force' and are the essence of war; 'the play of probability and chance within which the creative spirit is free to roam'; and 'its element of subordination, as an instrument of policy, which makes it subject to reason alone'.[63] No one of the three elements is continually dominant, not even policy. Clausewitz used a metaphor from physics to explore this relationship, likening each of the three to a magnet, with the theory of war suspended between them, as they both attracted and repelled each other. However, unlike many of the other triads which litter *On War* and are not necessarily intimately linked, this trinity, like the Christian trinity, really is three elements united in one. Clausewitz used the adjective *wunderlich* to describe it. Howard and Paret translate this as 'remarkable', but this understates the force of the epithet, which given its mystical connotations could be rendered more appropriately as 'wondrous' or even 'miraculous'.

Clausewitz then went on to associate each of these attributes with three components of the state at war. It was these, rather than the attributes themselves, that so appealed to Colin Powell and other Americans after the Vietnam War. The second, that linked to the issue of moral qualities, *Geist* and courage, was the province of the army and the military genius at its head. The third was the government, which by remaining detached from the battlefield directed policy along rational lines. The first, however, was an attribute of the *Volk*, the entire nation, since the passions which war kindles must already be present in the people.

The shift from the original trinity of moral attributes to a trinity of specific actors makes plain why the commentators on Clausewitz of the late twentieth century tended to privilege the political and rational over the passionate and popular. The second and subsidiary set are the tools of a nation that opts to wage war to achieve a specific set of objectives, not features of war itself. War involves reciprocity: even at its most rational it can never itself be an act of policy as it is the intention of the enemy to confound efforts to implement that policy. Put crudely, in war two trinities clash with each other, and it is the conflict between the three elements of each which generates the scope for friction and escalation. Where policy is pitted against passion, where hostility ousts rationality, the characteristics of war itself can subordinate and usurp those of the 'trinity'.

Until 1976 few Clausewitz scholars devoted much attention to this brief and underdeveloped section on the 'trinity'. Raymond Aron made it central to his study of Clausewitz, *Penser la guerre, Clausewitz*, but he concentrated on the rational element and neglected both the people themselves and their potential for irrationality. However, particularly since 1990 and the Cold War's end, the trinity has provided those anxious to prove Clausewitz's continuing relevance with plenty of food for thought. Many of these interpretations go far beyond what the text will bear, but such efforts are in part justified by Clausewitz's use of the word *mehr*, or 'mainly', when he links the passions to the people, the play of probability to the army, and the role of reason to the government. The qualification in the adverb allows for the possibility that the people can be rational, the army passionate, the government concerned with the play of probability and chance, and so on. Above all, he reintroduces the possibility that war can be elemental, rather than instrumental.

Clausewitz clearly says a great deal elsewhere in *On War* about the characteristics which he associates with the army, and a reasonable amount about the government and its policies. He seems to say less about passion or about the people who express it, and yet this is the element that has become central to the argument that future conflicts will not be fought by symmetrical armies within a European state system shaped by the balance of power – the wars which Clausewitz himself largely experienced and whose analysis dominated his writings – but will instead be waged by insurgents and non-state actors, using terrorism and ambush, dispersing rather than concentrating to fight.

Clausewitz regarded primitive peoples as possessed of a warlike spirit far greater than that of civilized peoples. Although he referred to Marathas, Tatars and Turks only in passing, he described Asia as a continent where 'a state of war is virtually permanent'.[64] One of the consequences of civilization was the loss of these warrior-like qualities, with the result that nations – like Prussia between 1763 and 1806 – became progressively less bold. Individual military genius, a quality not found in primitive societies, offset this decline in collective courage. Clausewitz thought that the

Russian general, Alexander Suvorov, was not up to the conduct of war which employed mass armies in developed countries because he had honed his skills fighting the Turks, a 'half-civilized people', whose wars were 'partial undertakings which achieved their effects as the sum of their parts rather than through their cohesion'.[65] Although dismissive of international law in moderating war, he did conclude that wars between civilized societies were less cruel and destructive than wars between savages: 'Savage peoples are ruled by passion, civilized peoples by the mind.'[66] Policy, being associated in the Clausewitzian trinity with reason, therefore had a greater field of influence within wars between civilized states. The implication here was that people were either passionately involved in war, but that in such wars policy and reason were marginalized, or that people were marginal and policy and reason dominant. But having suggested that peoples were not part of war's political dynamic, Clausewitz corrected himself. 'When whole communities go to war – whole peoples, and especially civilized peoples – the reason always lies in some political situation, and the occasion is always due to some political object [*Motiv*, not *Zweck*].'[67]

Even civilized peoples could be fired with passionate hatred, so combining depth of feeling and rationality. The main lesson of the French Revolution was that a people that was both civilized and passionate, and so politically aware, could create an army that was superior to the regular armies on which most of *On War*'s analysis focused.

Writing on the character of contemporary warfare in Book 3, chapter 17, Clausewitz reviewed the events of the later Napoleonic wars to show the 'enormous contribution the heart and temper of a nation can make to the sum total of its politics, war potential, and fighting strength'.[68] One of the examples to illustrate this triad – itself an anticipation of the trinity of Book 1, chapter 1 – was Prussia. After the treaty of Tilsit, Clausewitz and Gneisenau, inspired by the examples of Spain and Tyrol, had planned a national insurrection, intending to turn the idea of the nation in arms against France itself. In 1811, Clausewitz had filed a report on Silesia as the possible theatre for such a war,[69] and in 1813 the formation of the Landwehr had fulfilled the hopes of both of them for a popular rising. 'Prussia taught us in 1813', Clausewitz wrote in Book 3, 'that rapid efforts can increase an army's strength six times if we make use of a militia, and, what is more, that the militia can fight as well in foreign countries as at home.'[70] Advocating its retention after the peace, Clausewitz reminded Prussia that the Landwehr was superior in organization to the regular army it had possessed in the eighteenth century, precisely because it touched the entire people, infusing them with a warlike spirit, and enabling 'the element of war' to operate 'with all its raw natural power'.[71]

Despite his use of the epithet 'rapid' in his description of the events of 1813, Clausewitz was clear that a nation in arms could not be improvised, precisely because of the implicit contradiction between the peacetime avocations of civilized nations and the demands for boldness in war. France relied increasingly on long-service soldiers and foreign contingents during the course of the Napoleonic wars, and the result was that Napoleon had had to attack into Belgium in 1815, precisely because he could not reckon on enjoying any of the inherent benefits which popular passion gave to the defence. After its defeat at Waterloo, the French army – although falling back across its own country – was unsupported by the people: Clausewitz likened it to an army in a foreign land.[72]

Public opinion, already highlighted in his 1804 notes as an object in war, was identified as lying outside the army and independent of it. But, in the event of an invasion, the people might provide supplies and intelligence, while depriving the attacker of both. Their participation might even become active. Insurrectionary warfare, lauded by Clausewitz in 1809 in the light of events in Spain, showed how the spirit of the people could overcome the virtues of the regular army. Guerrillas were particularly effective in mountains and forests, geographical conditions which forced a regular army to disperse, so forfeiting its advantages of command and thus of military genius. Regulars preferred to fight in open country and seek battle; guerrillas spurned both. The value of insurrectionary or partisan war (Clausewitz used both titles) therefore lay within the relationship that most interested him, that between tactics and strategy. What partisans lacked in tactical effectiveness they gained through strategy. By avoiding battle they forced the enemy to disperse; the longer his line of communications, the more the opportunity for harassment and surprise. Thus they acted across the links between a field army and the theatre of war in which it was operating.[73]

Clausewitz refused to address the revolutionary implications of arming the people, rating the value of their contribution to the idea of national defence as more important than the consequences for domestic order. But this does not mean that in highlighting guerrilla war's role in linking tactics and strategy, Clausewitz neglected its contribution to the relationship between strategy and policy. Book 6, chapter 26, which was devoted to popular insurrection against an invader, is often read as demonstrating on the one hand Clausewitz's interest in the phenomenon and on the other his limited appreciation of its value. Because he saw it as ancillary to 'symmetrical' war between armies, he failed, or so the argument runs, to anticipate its potential to become free-standing in the way in which Martin van Creveld did in 1991. However, Clausewitz makes clear at the very beginning of the chapter that he was dealing with something that was both new in war and had the potential to become much bigger: 'A people's war in civilized Europe is a phenomenon of the nineteenth century.'[74]

'This sort of warfare', he wrote, 'is not as yet very common', and those who 'have been able to observe it for any length of time have not yet reported enough about it'.[75] The question that this remark prompts is whether Clausewitz himself intended to fill the gap in the literature even more fully than he did. The unfinished note on the manuscript of *On War* makes clear that Clausewitz saw his book at that stage as concerned with major war only.[76] He therefore recognized 'small war' as a subject worthy of separate study, and one possible implication is that, if he had lived longer, he himself might have undertaken such a work. This hypothesis rests on more than unsubstantiated speculation.

When Clausewitz joined the army in 1792, 'small war' carried very precise connotations. It encompassed the forms of fighting that took place away from the main battlefield, such as the protection of supplies, the harrying of outposts, and the collecting of intelligence. These responsibilities required select troops who were more reliable than the average soldier of the line, given the opportunities for desertion that detached duty presented, and who also showed more initiative and were probably better educated. In the wars on Europe's frontiers and in America, light cavalry and light infantry did more than screen the movements of the army's main body; they increasingly conducted a form of war that was independent and self-contained. Tactical flexibility, especially if it was elevated to strategic independence, carried implications for the democratization of an army which did not appeal to Frederick the Great or the more traditional officers of the Prussian army, but for those in the military reform movement it was the corollary of the political and social changes which armies were undergoing.

In 1810 Scharnhorst, who was planning popular resistance as the basis for Prussia to fight France, gave Clausewitz the task of lecturing on small war at the war school. Clausewitz's lecture notes constitute a sizeable body of work. His method was much more historical than abstract. He told his audience that too much recent writing lacked an understanding of war as it really was, and advised them to spurn 'the assimilation of rules by memory'.[77] He taught by way of case studies, including his own experience in 1793–4, whilst disarmingly acknowledging how limited it was. His principal references, and the reading he recommended to his students, were the works of Johann von Ewald and Andreas Emmerich, both Hessians who had served in the Seven Years War and in the American War of Independence.

At one level, therefore, Clausewitz was concerned to repeat the orthodoxies relating to small war as it had been understood in the eighteenth century. In part it was exactly what its title said it was – small because it involved fewer combatants. 'The strategy of small war is an area of tactics', he said; therefore the tactics of small war were also part of tactics, 'and so the whole of small war falls into tactics'.[78] The first part of his course covered outposts, and was consequently linked directly to the operations of major war, but the second dealt with partisans or the work of independent detachments. Even here, however, he reined in any inclination to see small war as a free-standing entity. When describing the role of partisans in pursuing a retreating enemy, he acknowledged that the implications of such action were strategic but concluded that in that case it no longer belonged in the realm of small war. The lectures were determinedly focused – like so much else that he wrote at this stage of his career – on tactical practice and therefore were, by his own lights, more susceptible to method than his condemnation of other theorists allowed for. His aim, he said, was to establish rules, albeit ones which were comprehensible and useable, and based on real events.[79]

The study of small war in the late eighteenth century was, however, also predicated on the assumption that it was a school of instruction for future commanders: indeed, that belief presumably underpinned the attention given to it at the Berlin war school in 1810. Clausewitz began his course by distinguishing it from the duties of the General Staff, which belonged to major war and were, in his word, mechanical. Small war was a matter of art and judgement, requiring cunning, flexibility and foresight: Clausewitz spoke of the 'free play of the spirit', using the same word, *Geist*, that he would later use of military genius.[80] Moreover, his examples did not stop short in 1794, but included references to the 'civil war' (his title) waged by French counter-revolutionaries in the Vendée against the Paris government in the mid-1790s, and the guerrilla wars conducted by the peoples of Tyrol and Spain – 'nations in arms' as he called them – against Napoleon in 1807–9.[81]

The latter proved inspirational for many German

nationalists, and Clausewitz's papers include a synopsis of the Peninsular War up until 1811. Here the tactics of small war acquired strategic and even political ends, and tied in with Clausewitz's preparations for anti-French resistance in Silesia. Ferdinand von Schill, who sustained partisan war against the French after the battle of Jena until his death in 1809, impressed both Clausewitz and Gneisenau. Schill had used the support of the local population to supply and hide his men, and Scharnhorst anticipated the formation of a home defence force which would wear no uniforms, would launch surprise attacks, and then melt back into the civilian community. These concepts underpinned the third of Clausewitz's political manifestos of February 1812, the document in which the tactical details of the war school lectures were fused with a Fichtean vision of national liberation. Calling for a levée en masse of the entire population aged eighteen to sixty, it argued that an insurgency could grow into a general war, in other words that small war could become a major war. Clausewitz acknowledged that such a conflict would be cruel, that 'the world trembles at the idea of a war of the people because it is more bloody than any other, that it seldom occurs without scenes of horror'. But, he asked, 'whose fault is that? Is it not the fault of those who drive others to the depths of desperation? They, not those on whom it has been forced, are to blame for its terrible consequences.[82] Small war, derived from eighteenth-century tactical precepts but employing terror and atrocities, coalesced with the idea of existential war.

Book 6, chapter 26, embraces this possibility, that wars of the future would be waged by a politically aware, passionate people, fighting for the independence of their nation, and not ready to accept the verdict of the battlefield. They would broaden and intensify 'the whole ferment which we call war'. A people's war (Clausewitz used the word *Volkskrieg*) was 'a consequence of the way in which in our day the elemental violence of war has burst its old artificial barriers'.[83] Its methods would be those of small war, 'nebulous and elusive; its resistance should never materialize as a concrete body, otherwise the enemy can direct sufficient force at its core, crush it, and take many prisoners'. But there would still be times when the people would have to concentrate, when 'the fog must thicken and form a dark and menacing cloud out of which a bolt of lightning may strike at any time'.[84]

Typically, for this stage of his writing, Clausewitz, having set up a proposition, advanced its counter. Such concentrations were more likely to be on the flanks of the enemy army, and this in turn implied a theatre of war where time and space were sufficiently extensive to force the enemy army to disperse, thus enhancing the opportunities for the partisans. Only in Russia did he deem the geographical conditions sufficiently appropriate for a national insurrection to achieve a crisis without the involvement of regular forces. Although Clausewitz called this insight realism, in fact it marked the consequence of reality's interplay with theory. Neither Prussia after 1806 nor France in 1814 had embraced a war of national liberation.

Clausewitz could not therefore elevate the idea of a *Volkskrieg* to a universal model for the future, and indeed he would have looked one-dimensional and incoherent even today had he done so. But as the peroration to chapter 26 revealed, with its summons to existential war, and its reflection of the much more intense realities of 1812 and 1813, Clausewitz recognized that political necessity could in practice override military common sense. The crisis in his thinking which his undated note and the note of 1827 reveal was prompted in part by his awareness that there was much more to war than 'major war', and that might be more true, not less so, in the future. Clausewitz's understanding of the nature of war anticipated that its three elements, the trinity, could radically change its character. His theory allowed for the possibility of 'new wars' to a much greater extent than Martin van Creveld and Mary Kaldor have recognized.

CONCLUSION

On War is a book about war in the present and the immediate past – both of them Clausewitz's, not ours. It is not overtly a book about the future of war. Yet this is how it is often read, and not without reason. Clausewitz's core problem, even if largely implicit, was the likely shape of wars to come. In 1827, using the past as the basis for his judgement, he decided that there were two sorts of war: wars of observation and wars of decision. Only rarely did he permit himself prognostication as to which would prevail in the future. Moreover, he was not consistent in what he said. In Book 6, chapter 28, he wrote that, 'One may predict that most wars will tend to revert to wars of observation.'[1] From the short-term perspective of, say, 1850, that looked to have been a reasonable expectation: during the revolutions that swept Europe in 1830 and 1848 armies watched the antics of neighbouring states more often than they intervened in them. But a hundred years later, in 1950, Clausewitz's conclusion in Book 8, chapter 3B, would look more prescient. Having reviewed the history of war up until Napoleon, when 'war, untrammelled by any conventional restraints, had broken loose in all its elemental fury', he asked himself the logical question: 'Will this be the case in the future?' 'From now on will every war in Europe be waged with the full resources of the state, and therefore have to be fought only over major issues that affect the people?' He refused to give a straight answer, but, ever the realist, he went on to acknowledge that 'once barriers – which in a sense consist only in man's ignorance of what is possible – are torn down, they are not so easily put up again'.[2]

Clausewitz's reluctance to be dogmatic on the shape of future war highlights an extraordinary gap in his perception of war's nature. He saw strategy as dependent on tactics. His reflections on tactics, which mirrored the debates of the day, were not particularly original. Should infantry be deployed in lines to maximize their firepower, or in columns for shock and mobility? Given the value of field artillery's firepower, how many guns could an army comfortably accommodate without jeopardizing its own mobility? What was the correct use of cavalry when it was vulnerable to the fire even of smoothbore weapons but remained vital to the exploitation of battlefield success?[3] In answering these questions, he inclined to favour the effects of firepower over shock. And yet, despite his own interests in mechanics and the physical sciences, he never explored the consequences of technological change either for firepower specifically or for war more generally. His discussion in Book 5, chapter 4, of how the three arms should be balanced in the composition of an army, dwelt on terrain more than technology as the determinant of the relative numbers of cavalry and artillery. By 1871, the principles of breech-loading and rifling were being applied both to the infantryman's firearm and to artillery; the railway had transformed the movements and supply of armies; and the telegraph had changed for ever the general's relationship to his political masters. Following his own logic, greater fire effect had the potential to alter tactics and therefore strategy, but when Clausewitz ruminated on the future of war, he saw change solely in social and political terms. There could be no more graphic indication of the influence of his own times: war in the age of Napoleon was transformed not by technology, but by social and political revolution.

Picking holes in *On War* is an easy game: it is massively Eurocentric; there is nothing on navies and little on economics. Written in an era when sovereign states enjoyed an unfettered right to resort to war, it neglected international law to an extent unacceptable since 1945. Moreover, Clausewitz contradicts himself, as this book has shown repeatedly. But that is also *On War*'s strength, its very essence and the reason for its longevity. It is a work in progress. Its unfinished nature should be a source not of frustration but of joy. Its author never stopped asking questions – not simply of his own conclusions but also of the methods by which he had reached them. The extraordinary fertility of his mind means that any attempt to seek uniformity and consistency in his arguments runs the risk of doing violence to their insights. Every generation has tended to look at what Clausewitz wrote in the light of its own preoccupations, but in using his thoughts in this way is always in danger of treating the text selectively. That in itself is neither illegitimate nor inappropriate, but by the same token no one school can claim the monopoly of wisdom in its interpretation of Clausewitz's work. Freezing his thought at any stage of its development, even the allegedly sacrosanct one represented by Book 1, chapter 1, creates the danger both that the very richness of the author's mind will be lost, and that *On War* itself will be consigned to premature oblivion.

The introduction showed the frequency with which Clausewitz has been declared dead, not just since 1990, but also after 1918 and 1945. The chapters which followed demonstrated how many axioms derived from *On War* can be countered by others, also drawn from the same text. Clausewitz knew full well that policy can expand war as well as limit it; that absolute war can approach a reality as well as form a theoretical concept; and that the people are as central to war as are the government and army. Clausewitz's maturation was marked not by his making up his mind on these issues, but by his growing commitment to the methodology of dialectics. Clausewitz himself – to commit the very sin of selective quotation – gave the best riposte to those who seek to pigeon-hole him: war, he said, was 'a true chameleon, because it adapts its nature to meet each case'.[4] But then, of course, he went on to qualify the statement.

NOTES

Introduction

1 Colin Powell, with Joseph Persico, *My American Journey*, New York, Random House, 1995, pp. 207–8.

2 Harry G. Summers, Jr., *On Strategy: A critical analysis of the Vietnam war*, Novato, CA, Presidio, 1981, pp. 4, 6.

3 Christopher Bassford, *Clausewitz in English*, New York, Oxford University Press, 1994, p. 204.

4 Russell Weigley, 'The American military and the principle of civilian control from McClellan to Powell', *Journal of Military History*, 57, 5 (special issue), 1993, p. 29.

5 Tommy Franks, with Malcolm McConnell, *American Soldier*, New York, Regan Books, 2004, p. 165.

6 Clausewitz, *Ausgewählte militärische Schriften*, Berlin, Militärverlag der deutschen Demokratischen Republik, 1981, edited by Gerhard Förster and Dorothea Schmidt, p. 372.

7 Clausewitz, 'Der Feldzug von 1796 in Italien', in *Sämtliche Schriften 'Vom Kriege'*, Mundus, 1999, Band 2, p. 17.

8 Quoted by Ami-Jacques Rapin, *Jomini et la stratégie: une approche historique de l'oeuvre*, Lausanne, Payot, 2002, p. 205.

9 Ulrich Marwedel, *Carl von Clausewitz. Persönlichkeit und*

Wirkungsgeschichte seiner Werkes bis 1918, Boppard am Rhein, Harald Boldt, 1978, p. 117.

10 Gerhard Ritter, *The Sword and the Scepter: The problem of militarism in Germany*, 4 vols, Coral Gables, Florida, University of Miami Press, 1969–72, vol. I, pp. 194–5.

11 Ibid., vol. I, p. 195.

12 Daniel J. Hughes (ed.), *Moltke on the Art of War: Selected writings*, Novato, CA, Presidio, 1993, p. 47.

13 G. G. [Gilbert], *Essais de critique militaire*, Paris, *La Nouvelle Revue*, 1890, p. 20; from an article first published in *La Nouvelle Revue* in 1887.

14 Ferdinand Foch, *The Principles of War*, London, Chapman and Hall, 1918; first published in France, 1903, pp. 4–5, 42.

15 Basil Liddell Hart, *Foch: The Man of Orleans*, London, Eyre and Spottiswoode, 1931, p. 21.

16 Basil Liddell Hart, *The Ghost of Napoleon*, London, Faber & Faber, 1933, p. 122.

17 Erich Ludendorff, *The Nation at War*, London, Hutchinson, n.d., p. 24.

18 Ibid., p. 23.

19 Hans-Adolf Jacobsen, *Karl Haushofer – Leben und Werk*, 2 vols, Boppard am Rhein, Harald Boldt, 1979, p. 376.

20 Clausewitz, *Vom Kriege*, abridged edition edited by Friedrich von Cochenhausen, Leipzig, Insel, 1937, p. 5.

21 Bemard Semmel (ed.), *Marxism and the Science of War*, Oxford, Oxford University Press, 1981, p. 66. The German word is *Witz*, which Semmel translates as 'brilliance'.

22 Ibid., p. 69.

23 Olaf Rose, *Carl von Clausewitz. Wirkungsgeschichte seines*

Werkes Russland und der Sowjetunion 1836–1991, Munich, Oldenbourg, 1995, p. 205.

24 David Holloway, *The Soviet Union and the Arms Race*, New Haven, Yale University Press, 1983, p. 165.

25 Ritter originally published these views in 1943 in the *Historisches Zeitschrift*, see P. M. Baldwin, 'Clausewitz in Nazi Germany', *Journal of Contemporary History*, XVI (1981), p. 19.

26 Michael Mandelbaum, *The Nuclear Question: The United States and nuclear weapons 1946–1976*, Cambridge, Cambridge University Press, 1979, pp. 3–4.

27 Stewart L. Murray, *The Reality of War: An introduction to 'Clausewitz'*, London, Hugh Rees, 1909, p. 10.

Chapter 1

1 *On War*, p. 61. Published by Maria von Clausewitz in her Introduction to the original edition, and as a separate note by Howard and Paret.

2 Karl Linnebach (ed.), *Karl u. Marie von Clausewitz. Ein Lebensbild in Briefen und Tagebuchblättern*, Berlin, Martin Warneck, 1917, p. 110.

3 Ibid., p. 138.

4 Ibid., p. 135.

5 *On War*. 8, 3B, Jolles, p. 584.

6 Or he said he was: the church register says 1 July. See Gerhard Förster, *Carl von Clausewitz*, Berlin, Militärverlag der deutschen Demokratischen Republik, 1983, p. 1.

7 *On War*, p. 66.

8 Hans Rothfels, *Carl von Clausewitz. Politik und Krieg*, Berlin, Dümmler, 1920; new edition, Bonn, Dümmler, 1980, p. 102.

9 Clausewitz, *Vom Kriege*, Book 6, chapter 23, p. 665; this is omitted or moderated in all English translations.

10 Linnebach, *Karl u. Marie Clausewitz*, p. 96.

11 Ibid., p. 83. The reference is to a fictional character in Friedrich Schiller's trilogy, *Wallenstein* (1798–9); Piccolomini is the spokesman of Schiller's philosophical and moral position, reflecting the influence of Kant.

12 Clausewitz, *Preussen in seiner grossen Katastrophe*, first published 1880; reprinted, Vienna, Karolinger, 2001, p. 19.

13 Comte de Guibert, *A General Essay on Tactics*, 2 vols, London, 1781, vol. I, p. viii. For Clausewitz's use of it, see Clausewitz, *Schriften-Aufsätze-Studien-Briefe*, 2 vols, Göttingen, Vandenhoeck & Ruprecht, 1966–90, edited by Werner Hahlweg, vol. 1, pp. 710–11.

14 *On War*, 6, 30, p. 515.

15 Ibid., 6, 30, p. 518.

16 Scharnhorst, 'Entwicklung der allgemeinen Ursachen des Glücks der Franzosen in dem Revolutionskriege und insbesondere in dem Feldzüge von 1794', Gerhard von Scharnhorst, *Ausgewählte militärische Schriften*, hg. Hansjürgen Usczeck and Christa Gudzent, Berlin, Militärverlag der deutschen Demokratischen Republik, 1986, p. 105.

17 Linnebach, *Karl u. Maria Clausewitz*, p. 128.

18 Ibid., p. 85. Clausewitz used the word 'Geist', which means both intellect and spirit; the problems of translating this word, so important to Clausewitz and used by him so often, are discussed below, pp. 92–4, 126.

19 Clausewitz, *Strategie aus dem Jahr 1804 mit Zusätzen von 1808 und 1809*, Hamburg, Hanseatische Verlagsanstalt, 1937, edited by Eberhard Kessel, p. 56.

20 'Considérations sur la manière de faire la guerre à la France'
    in Clausewitz, *Schriften*, edited by Werner Hahlweg, vol. I,
    pp. 58–63.

21 Clausewitz, *Preussen in seiner grossen Katastrophe*, pp. 9, 53,
    72–3, 78.

22 Linnebach, *Karl u. Maria Clausewitz*, p. 59.

23 Clausewitz, *Preussen in seiner grossen Katastrophe*, p. 20.

24 Linnebach, *Karl u. Maria Clausewitz*, p. 65.

25 Clausewitz, 'Historische Briefe über die grossen
    Kriegereignisse im Oktober 1806' in Clausewitz, *Ausgewählte
    militärische Schriften*, Berlin, Militäverlag der deutschen
    Demokratischen Republik, 1981, edited by Gerhard Förster
    and Dorothea Schmidt, p. 73.

26 Ibid., p. 75.

27 Linnebach, *Karl u. Maria Clausewitz*, p. 71.

28 Werner Hahlweg, *Clausewitz. Soldat-Politiker-Denker*,
    Göttingen, Musterschmidt-Verlag, 1969, p. 33.

29 Clausewitz to Gneisenau, 17 June 1811, in Clausewitz,
    Schriften, edited by Hahlweg, p. 645; see *On War*, 2, p. 133.

30 Linnebach, *Karl u. Maria Clausewitz*, p. 226.

31 Clausewitz, *Schriften*, edited by Hahlweg, vol. 1, pp. 66–90,
    here pp. 79, 81, 89.

32 Ibid., p. 638.

33 Clausewitz, *Historical and Political Writings*, Princeton,
    Princeton University Press, 1992, edited and translated by
    Peter Paret and Daniel Moran, p. 290; for the full and
    annotated text, see Clausewitz, *Schriften*, vol. 1, pp. 682–750.
    Hahlweg calls these documents collectively
    'Bekenntnisdenkschrift', which could be translated as a
    'statement of confession'; Paret and Moran settle for

'political declaration'; Clausewitz himself gave them no title.

34 Adolf Hitler, *Mein Kampf*, London, Hurst & Blackett, 1939, pp. 544–5, 1938, pp. 759–61.

35 *On War*, 6, 26, p. 483.

36 Clausewitz, *Historical and Political Writings*, p. 300.

37 Clausewitz, *Strategie aus dem Jahr 1804*, p. 42.

38 Clausewitz, *Historical and Political Writings*, p. 201; see also Clausewitz, *The Campaign of 1812 in Russia*, first published 1843; reprinted New York, Da Capo, 1995, p. 252; *On War*, 8, 9, pp. 626–7.

39 Clausewitz, *Campaign of 1812*, p. 253.

40 Ibid., pp. 95–8, 253–5; *On War*, 3, 12, p. 208; 4, 12, p. 266; 5, 12, p. 323; 5, 14, p. 336; 6, 8, p. 385.

41 Clausewitz, *Campaign of 1812*, p. 14; *On War*, 8, 8, p. 615.

42 To Gneisenau, 7 November 1812, in Clausewitz, *Schriften*, edited by Hahlweg, vol. 2, p. 131.

43 Linnebach, *Karl u. Marie von Clausewitz*, p. 304.

44 Writing to Marie, 29 November 1812, in ibid., p. 305.

45 Clausewitz, *Ausgewählte militärische Schriften*, ed. Förster and Schmidt, p. 306.

46 On the two battles and their contexts, see T. C. W. Blanning, *The French Revolutionary Wars 1787–1802*, London, Arnold, 1996, and David Gates, *The Napoleonic Wars 1803–1815*, London, Arnold, 1997.

47 Clausewitz, *Ausgewählte Militärische Schriften.*, p. 256.

48 Linnebach, *Karl u. Marie von Clausewitz*, p. 341.

49 Ibid., p. 365.

50 Clausewitz, 'Our military institutions', in *Historical and Political Writings*, p. 317.

51 Clausewitz, 'On the political advantages and disadvantages

of the Prussian Landwehr', in *Historical and Political Writings*, p. 332.

52 Clausewitz, *Schriften*, edited by Hahlweg, vol. 2, pp. 592–3.

53 Linnebach, *Karl u. Marie von Clausewitz*, p. 447.

Chapter 2

1 Clausewitz, *Ausgewählte Briefe an Marie von Clausewitz und Gneisenau*, Berlin, Verlag der Nation, 1953, p. 264.

2 *On War* (Howard and Paret edition), p. 66.

3 Peter Paret, 'The genesis of *On War*', ibid., pp. 6–7.

4 Ibid., 5, 9, p. 313.

5 *On War*, p. 67.

6 *On War*, p. 70.

7 Clausewitz, *Schriften*, edited by Werner Hahlweg, vol. 2, pp. 625–7. See also Walther Malmsten Schering, *Die Kriegsphilosophie von Clausewitz*, Hamburg, Hanseatische Verlagsanstalt, 1935, pp. 24–6.

8 *On War*, 8, 9, p. 636.

9 *On War*, Jolles, pp. xxix–xxx.

10 Clausewitz, *Strategie aus dem Jahr 1804*, pp. 51–2.

11 *On War*, 6, 30, p. 515; 7, 22, p. 570; 8, 2, p. 580; 8, 3, p. 583; 8, 3, p. 592.

12 Peter Paret, *Clausewitz and the State*, Oxford, Oxford University Press, 1976, p. 330, suggests a chronology, which I have only partly followed. The dates suggested for the study of 1806 are contradicted by the introduction to the French edition of 1903, *Notes sur la Prusse dans sa grande catastrophe. 1806*, Paris, R. Chapelot, 1903, pp. 2–3.

13 Clausewitz, 'Die Feldzüge von 1799 in Italien und Schweiz', in *Sämtliche Schriften 'Vom Kriege'*, Band 2, p. 317.

14 Clausewitz, *Principles of War*, London, John Lane, The Bodley Head, 1943, edited by Hans W. Gatzke, p. 54.

15 Andreas Herberg-Rothe, *Das Rätsel Clausewitz*, Munich, Wilhelm Fink, 2001, pp. 27–49.

16 Azar Gat, *The Origins of Military Thought from the Enlightenment to Clausewitz*, Oxford, Oxford University Press, 1989, pp. 199–252.

17 Clausewitz, *Two Letters on Strategy*, edited and translated by Peter Paret and Daniel Moran, US Army War College, 1984; see also Peter Paret, *Understanding War*, Princeton, Princeton University Press, 1992, pp. 123–9.

18 *On War*, 6, 8, p. 389; Howard and Paret translate this passage as though it refers to the whole work, and thus minimize the innovatory point of the observation, but Clausewitz referred to '*unseres Buches*', which could refer specifically to Book 6.

19 *On War*, p. 62.

20 This discussion is informed by the outlines for the book contained in Clausewitz, *Schriften*, edited by Hahlweg, vol. 2, pp. 623–716, and especially pp. 675–80, an outline for Book 8.

21 *On War*, 2, 2, p. 136; also 2, 5, pp. 168–9.

22 *On War*, 4, 11 and 12 (Graham edition), 1, pp. 289, 292. Howard and Paret, here and elsewhere in this book, elect not to translate '*System*' as system.

23 *On War*, 3, 14; this is an adapted version of Graham, vol. I, p. 221, which gets nearer to the original German than any other translation.

24 *On War*, 4, 12, p. 267; 5, 7, p. 304; 5, 9, p. 312; 5, 13, p. 328; 5, 15, p. 342; 5, 17, p. 348; 5, 18, p. 353; 6, 2, p. 360; 6, 4, p. 368; 6, 18, pp. 433–5.

25 Ibid., 5, 17, p. 348.

26 Ibid., 4, 4, p. 234; 4, 9, p. 250; 4, 10, p. 253.

27 Ibid., 5, 2, p. 280.

28 Because Howard and Paret frequently prefer to translate 'philosophisch' as scientific, the point is lost in this translation; Clausewitz eschews '*wissenschaftlich*', which is what their rendering implies. See Werner Hahlweg, 'Philosophice und Theorie bei Clausewitz' in Eberhard Wagemann and Joachim Niemeyer (eds), *Freiheit ohne Krieg?*, Bonn, Dümmler 1980.

29 *On War*, p. 63.

30 Herberg-Rothe, *Das Rätsel Clausewitz*, pp. 92–3.

31 Ibid., pp. 107–21; Paret, *Clausewitz and the State*, p. 316; Raymond Aron, *Penser la guerre, Clausewitz*, 2 vols, Paris, Gallimard, 1976, vol. 1, pp. 360–5; Gat, *Origins of Military Thought*, pp. 230–35.

32 Linnebach, *Karl u. Marie von Clausewitz*, pp. 154–5.

33 Clausewitz, *Historical and Political Writings*, p. 282.

34 Clausewitz, *Strategie aus dem Jahr 1804*, pp. 40–41, 76; see also *On War*, 2, 2, p. 145.

35 Rothfels, *Carl von Clausewitz*, p. 107; see also pp. 130–31.

36 Werner Hahlweg, *Clausewitz. Soldat-Politiker-Denker*, p. 37.

37 He does use it in Book 1, chapter 1, para 3, suggesting that he perhaps planned to return to it as the more rational Clausewitz manifested himself towards the end of his life, but the context is not specifically to do with the attributes of the commander.

38 Clausewitz, *Geist und Tat*, Stuttgart, Alfred Kröner, 1941, edited by Walther Malmsten Schering, pp. 153–78; see Gat, *Origins of Military Thought*, pp. 175–84.